To my mother and the memory of my father

Political Corruption in Africa

ROBERT WILLIAMS
Lecturer in Politics,
University of Durham

Gower

Published by
Gower Publishing Company Limited,
Gower House, Croft Road, Aldershot, Hampshire, England.

Gower Publishing Company
Old Post Road, Brookfield, Vermont 05036, USA

British Library Cataloguing in Publication Data

Williams, Robert,
  Political corruption in Africa.
  1. Corruption (in politics) —— Africa,
  Sub-Saharan
  I. Title
  320.967   JQ1879.A15

  ISBN 0-566-00794-0

Printed and bound in Great Britain by
Blackmore Press, Shaftesbury, Dorset

Contents

Acknowledgements

My major and obvious debt is to the community of scholars who have transformed the study of both African politics and political corruption in the past twenty-five years. The references partly indicate the extent of my debt, but only those who have followed a similar academic path will appreciate its true proportions. In seminars, conferences and conversations in Africa, Australia, Britain and Brazil, I have rehearsed and revised most of the arguments in this book and I am extremely grateful to all who offered advice and criticism.

For assistance on a research visit to Zambia, I would like to thank Mr. David Moon and, for help with Kenyan sources, I owe a debt to Dr. Cherry Gertzel. I gratefully acknowledge the assistance of the University of Durham in providing travel grants and sabbatical leave to further my research. The camera ready copy was prepared by Mrs. Dorothy Anson with valuable assistance from Mrs. Jean Richardson. The production of the book owes a great deal to Mrs. Anson's initiative, drive and determination.

Although I am grateful for all the encouragement I have received, I must emphasise my particular debt to my wife, Elisabeth, for her enthusiastic and unfailing support. My children, Rachel, Rebecca, Abigail and Robert have all contributed their own quota of encouragement and distraction, but I know they share their father's relief that 'the book' is no longer an intrusion into family life.

Despite the advice and assistance I have received, I am acutely conscious that the faults and errors which remain are my responsibility.

Robert Williams
Durham, April 1986.

1 Introduction

A senior British civil servant was visiting a government department in a West African country when he became puzzled by his guide's habit of calling out sums of money as they passed each official's office. Puzzlement turned to outrage when he discovered the amounts represented the going rate for bribing each official. Accustomed to the impeccable standards of the British civil service, the visitor exclaimed 'Good God! Are there no honest men left in this department?' His guide thought for a moment and replied, 'One or two, but they're very expensive!'

Although corruption is neither peculiar to Africa nor peculiarly African, it may be tempting to believe that the above tale is more than apocryphal. Corruption is popularly viewed as the outstanding characteristic of African public life (1) and, if the accuracy of the perception is sometimes open to question, the expectations engendered by such attitudes sometimes encourages foreign visitors to expect and detect bribery in almost any encounter with African officials. An over-developed sensitivity to corruption can produce odd behaviour as, for example, when an immigration officer in Accra casually asked a visiting British businessman the time and, without a word, the visitor unstrapped his watch and slipped it into the official's breast pocket.

But while travellers' tales may be both atypical and exaggerated, few scholars doubt that corruption is an important and prominent feature of political, bureaucratic and business (2) life in tropical Africa. This is not, of course, to suggest that corruption is either insignificant or unobtrusive in other parts of the Third World or even that corruption is exclusively or predominantly a feature of underdevelopment. To accept that corruption is pandemic does not preclude the recognition of significant variations in the origins, incidence and importance of corruption in different regions or countries. If a mature, developed democracy like the United States regularly produces revelations of corruption in local, state and federal politics, it has not yet been seriously argued that it has reached levels likely to threaten national bankruptcy, to paralyse government or to destroy the American public's belief in the legitimacy and efficacy of their political system. (3) Conversely, many students of African affairs suspect that corruption does have profound and damaging effects on economic performance, administrative effectiveness and governmental authority. Thus, corruption in Africa merits serious attention not just because it appears more prevalent than it is, for example, in Britain, but because of the widespread perception that it has major consequences for political and economic development.

Different political and economic systems facilitate or impede the growth of corruption in different ways, but there is some evidence to suggest that many African countries display precisely those combinations of institutional and political characteristics and socio-economic conditions most likely to ensure that corruption will flourish. Much of this study is concerned to explore such characteristics and conditions to ascertain both how they emerged and how they have helped to shape the form and level of corruption in different societies. At the outset, it should be stressed that the chapters which follow neither attempt to formulate a general theory or law of political corruption nor purport to offer an encyclopaedic account of corruption in Africa. To attempt the latter would be foolhardy given our very limited knowledge about corruption and to attempt the former suggests that differences in historical development and political and economic circumstances make no material difference to the nature, growth or spread of corrupt practices. If it is imprudent to reject the possibility of making law-like statements about political corruption, it may contribute to academic energy-saving to point out that political scientists have enjoyed little success in similar quests in other areas of their discipline.

This study is therefore selective rather than exhaustive in its treatment of corruption and it eschews those forms of taxonomy which purport to assign all aspects of corruption to their appropriate pigeon-holes. Corruption resists simple classification and taxonomies often cloud as well as clarify issues by giving the impression that frequently chaotic or amorphous situations possess unlikely degrees of order and structure. (4)   But if this study does not offer a general theory or a comprehensive framework for explaining corruption, it does try to identify and address the principal difficulties which impede the formulation of such theories and frameworks.   It draws particular attention to the need to identify corruption and ascertain reliable information about it, to locate the place and role of corruption both in different explanatory frameworks and in particular African contexts, to trace the causal flows and influences which shape the consequences of corruption and to chart the environmental factors which encourage its growth and impede its control.

The structure of the book reflects the above concerns and needs little in the way of justification or elaboration.   The study of corruption has proved something of a conceptual and methodological minefield, or perhaps more accurately, a bed of quicksand, and the first task of the book is to negotiate a safe path across and, where necessary, to skirt around it.   Thus, the next chapter considers the variety of meanings attributed to corruption, evaluates attempts to explain its significance and explores the implications for political analysis presented by the theoretical and definitional discussion.   At this stage, it may simply be observed that different definitions direct attention to different lines of inquiry and, whether corruption is judged in terms of illegality, immorality, unpopularity or by some other standard, the choice of definition reflects the focus and purpose of each analyst.   When what is termed corruption is perceived as isolated, infrequent, and deviant behaviour, it may be analysed with a conceptual armoury which would prove difficult to utilise in situations where corruption is endemic and pervasive. (5) Students of corruption employ a number of different approaches ranging from anthropological and sociological investigations of traditional 'gift-giving' practices through historical, institutional and psychological studies to economic analyses.   Within subject specialisms, ideological differences often have a major impact, for example, liberal economists tend to focus on the virtue and power of market forces while more radical analysts tend to emphasise the processes and consequences of capital accumulation in dependent societies. (6)   Thus different perspectives and priorities ensure analytical diversity and hence there is little prospect of agreement on the one approach to, or definition of, corruption which would reduce student perplexity. The issues pertaining to the incidence of corruption resist simple straightforward resolution, not just because of the variety of competing preconceptions its analysts bring to their material, but because African states display considerable political, economic and social diversity.

If   explanations   of   corruption   are   rarely   unequivocal   or uncontentious, there is some consensus that contemporary corruption has at least some of its roots in the past. The nature and identity of these roots may be matters of debate, but the third chapter in this book represents an effort to trace the major factors of modern African history which have accelerated or facilitated the growth of corruption. It focuses, in particular, on the colonial period both because it was largely instrumental in introducing modern Western principles of official conduct and because colonialism had an undeniably powerful influence on political structures, practices and aspirations.

The purpose is not to 'blame' wicked colonial rulers for corrupting innocent Africans, but rather to address the varying mixture of impositions and rewards, constraints and opportunities, which made the state in Africa the focus of aspiration without engendering any widespread sense of loyalty or legitimacy. It examines the style and tenor of colonial rule, the degree and form of political and economic inequality it generated and the accommodations it reached with many aspiring African nationalists. The 'wind of change' may have dispersed Africa's European masters and dispelled some of the myths of racial superiority, but the wind was not often strong enough to change economic realities, transform administrative structures or to mobilize politically more than a fraction of the population. On independence, African governments were commonly saddled with unbalanced and underdeveloped economies, inadequate and unskilled bureaucracies and an avalanche of popular demands for services and opportunities partly triggered by the unrealistic promises of nationalist politicians. Under the weight of economic, political and administrative pressures, something had to give. Too often, it seemed that, in order to protect their own positions, the political elite effectively raised the drawbridge and severed what few lines of accountability the elaborate but largely cosmetic independence constitutions provided. The castle gate was fortified and defended and access was increasingly only allowed to those who could pay the admission charges. Inevitably, such circumstances accelerated the growth of a class of intermediaries and fixers who knew which doors to open and which guards to bribe.

If the recent historical experience of Africa has guaranteed the political and economic centrality of the state, it has also shaped the way in which the machinery of government functions. Chapter Four examines in some detail the impact of various political and administrative arrangements and their likely consequences for corruption in contemporary Africa. It focuses, in part, on the relationship between administrative efficiency and corruption and discusses the nature and direction of the causal influences which impair administrative performance. The issues are complex, but the analysis suggests that, while corruption is often blamed for bureaucratic delay and incompetence, there are a variety of other important factors at work. Similarly, if corruption grows partly because of administrative inefficiency, it also grows for other reasons.

The purpose is not only to analyse the organisational and structural considerations which shape the role and impact of corruption in governmental processes, but to describe the main forms and mechanisms of corruption. The latter task involves both locating the political and administrative arenas where corruption most frequently occurs and, in occupational terms, (7) identifying the major participants. If some forms of corruption are simple, direct, bilateral transactions, others involve networks of complex, indirect and intangible deferred understandings. In other words, corruption may be crude and obvious or sophisticated and subtle, it may be petty and trivial or gigantic and profoundly significant.

The major scandals attract, by definition, the greatest publicity and popular reaction and the discussion of such scandals is linked to the character and policies of African governments. It focuses, in particular, on the African state as 'import-export agency' and the attendant problems of smuggling, shortages and currency manipulation. Two major Nigerian scandals are examined in some detail (8) to reveal the similarities between different examples of large-scale corruption and to emphasise the extent of their impact on Nigerian finances. The conclusion to the chapter brings together the elements of organisational structure and process, the pressures of economic constraints and the preferred policy choices which have combined to produce the prominent and prevalent forms of corruption in Africa.

But if the forms, techniques or mechanisms of corruption seem fairly constant, the role it plays in the political and economic life of different African states varies considerably. Thus, to explore the anatomy and physiology of corruption, without identifying the particular species and examining its origins, is to limit the analysis to broad general observations. But general observations are often insensitive to environmental variables and, therefore, Chapter Five is explicitly concerned to investigate the differing causes, catalysts and configurations of corruption in different types of political regime.

When factor endowments are disparate and political experiences are diverse, it suggests that simple models of corruption in Africa will not suffice. The regimes analysed in Chapter Five not only vary in their historical development, economic resources and political institutions, but in their populations, areas, and geo-political locations. They range from competitive party systems to one-party states to military regimes. In ideological terms, they range from capitalist to Marxist and conservative to

radical. Over time, many African states have experienced a
variety of different structures of political control but the
overriding impression is one of fragility and impermanence. Not
only have some states experienced chronic instability, but even
where a single party or ruler has been in power since
independence, as in Kenya and Zambia, the leadership's
preoccupation with continuity is strikingly evident. In unstable
environments, much political effort is dissipated in appeasing
warring factions, forging or renewing alliances, coopting or
coercing rivals and opponents and otherwise defending the castle
of state against intruders and usurpers. In the struggle to acquire
or maintain political supremacy, those with access to the state's
power and resources are likely to exploit them by whatever means
are necessary to achieve their ends. When authorised by the
highest political authority, such activity forms part of spoils
systems sanctioned by legal codes but, when practised by rivals
and subordinates, it is likely to be condemned as evidence of
corruption, nepotism or 'tribalism'.

The political and economic diversity of Africa ensures that the
role corruption plays varies according to circumstance and this
same diversity effectively excludes the possibility that any one
magic potion or set of reforms will have the same impact in very
different political contexts. Chapter Six addresses the problems
of reducing or controlling the level of corruption and evaluates
the effectiveness of some of the more common remedial
approaches. The methods used to control corruption vary according
to how seriously the problem is regarded and whether the
treatment is likely to prove damaging to the status and security
of leadership groups. Corruption is frequently employed as a form
of political abuse or accusation and responses to such charges are
bound, at least in part, to be calculated in terms of political
advantage. Political leaders are not always disinterested seekers
after truth and the frequent employment of judicial or
quasi-judicial inquiries into corruption does not constitute proof of
honorable intentions. In practice, such inquiries may indicate a
preoccupation with public relations rather than a commitment to
curb corruption.

Different prescriptions for controlling corruption seem to reflect
the academic disciplines, the ideological perspectives or the
material concerns of their sponsors. Where the commitment to
controlling corruption is not in doubt, the choice of remedies is
constrained by the desire to pursue other objectives. (9) The
range of choice is therefore limited by the need to reconcile
anti-corruption measures with other regime goals. If corruption
produces a supply of essential goods, only a naive or foolhardy
government would consider breaking the supply chain and risking
popular revolt. To the moralist, corruption is always an evil, but
political leaders recognise that it is sometimes preferable to the

likely alternatives.

The primary issue in combating corruption seems to be whether it can be treated as a superficial blemish or whether it requires a more fundamental approach. This study attempts to show that corruption flourishes under certain conditions and it would seem to follow that, as in medicine, the holistic approach is to be recommended. Altering the environment of the patient may prove more significant in treating the condition than addressing the more conspicuous symptoms. Treating the symptoms without tackling the underlying conditions which give rise to the symptoms is unlikely to produce lasting cures. (10) But this is to assume that those responsible for the patients actually want them to get better and, in many cases, such assumptions are unjustified. If full health were restored, it is always possible that many of Africa's political doctors would be at risk from their patients. In such cases, powerful vested interests combine to impede and delay the patient's recovery.

The titles of books often promise more than they deliver and this study is no exception. Some of the more obvious omissions, for example, the lack of any analysis of corruption in South or North Africa, are deliberate and reflect the limitations and interests of the author. Other omissions are the result of considerations of space and balance, for example, the range of cases examined in Chapter Five to illustrate different patterns of corruption. But many omissions and deficiencies are attributable to the nature of the subject and to the limitations of the available conceptual armoury. Corruption does not lend itself to easy identification, categorisation or measurement. If its incidence is sometimes hard to detect, its consequences are often difficult to disentangle.

This book proceeds on the basis that corruption in Africa is not an infrequent exceptional phenomenon which can, for analytical purposes, be abstracted and isolated from the environments in which it occurs. But rather it stresses that the growth of corruption is the product of wider historical, political and economic processes and that its causes, consequences and cures all need to be understood in their appropriate contexts. If corruption is integral to, rather than appendage of, African public life, it can only be properly comprehended within a broader understanding of the character of political and economic activity in Africa.

The lesson is that whether the concern is to trace the patterns of corruption in different African societies or to assess the efficacy of alternative strategies for controlling corruption, the focus of inquiry needs to be broad rather than narrow. The historical development, the political character, and the economic experiences of African societies help shape the contexts from which corruption springs and therefore comprise an essential part of this inquiry. In a brief compass, it is particularly difficult to do adequate justice to the diversity of regimes in Africa, but this study recognises that, if corruption is partly a symptom of more or less common economic dilemmas, its form and impact largely derive from particular historical circumstances and from specific policy choices.

In charting the origins of corruption, in describing its different structures and mechanisms and in evaluating methods of control, the arguments in this book traverse the academic preserves of different disciplines and area specialists and, in so doing, it is perhaps inevitable that some of the judgements and conclusions will provoke a critical response. If this is the case, it is unavoidable. The book is about Africa or, more accurately, about most of the countries of tropical and southern Africa and is not intended as a regional or single country study. Readers with a special interest in, or knowledge of, a particular country may perhaps be dissatisfied with my cursory analysis and inexcusable omissions. But my purpose has not been to write a set of exhaustive and comprehensive case studies of individual countries, partly because such a task seems to be outside the competence of any single scholar and partly because my concern is to explore to what extent the issues and problems are general ones. There are already some monographs on corruption in particular countries and, to my knowledge, several others are in preparation. Such studies may partly compensate for the deficiencies and omissions of this study, but they are not substitutes for it because their concerns are essentially parochial.

This book has no special ideological or methodological axes to grind and therefore it is not concerned to use a discussion of corruption to demonstrate the inevitable or obvious superiority of one dogma or political model over another. It is no part of my purpose to argue that corruption is the peculiar province of any one kind of regime or to assert that its effective control requires any one set of political and economic reforms. It may be, as we shall see, that certain regimes have displayed a marked propensity to corruption and that certain remedial treatments have conspicuously failed in particular cases. But this is not to argue that any particular type of regime is bound to be corrupt or that a particular reform proposal will always be ineffective.

The prolonged study of any political subject tends to encourage scholars to exaggerate its importance in order to justify their time and effort. Thus, the suggestion here that political corruption is an important and, on occasion, a dominant feature of African public life will come as no surprise. But it will also become clear that the extent or significance of corruption is not always what political leaders and their opponents say it is. The charge of corruption often has political reverberations extending far outside courts of law and serves, on occasion, to justify diverse forms of insurrection, intolerance and oppression. Thus, political corruption is important not only because of its consequences for the conduct of public affairs, but because it serves as a scapegoat or justification for conduct that would otherwise prove difficult to explain or defend.

If the importance of corruption in Africa is almost beyond dispute, its analysis remains problematic. Corruption lacks the precision, definition and cohesion of some other political topics. Analysis is difficult because corruption permeates political structures and their interstices rather than stands apart from them and because its often clandestine character resists close inspection and quantitative analysis. When access to the raw material is so limited, attempts to distinguish between, for example, extortion and bribery are fraught with difficulty. But such distinctions may not be crucial to understanding the role corruption plays in particular African societies for both extortion and bribery, when practised on a regular and extensive basis, suggest certain conclusions about the polities within which they occur.

It seems clear, despite the analytical difficulties, that corruption has something to do with the pre-eminence of the state in Africa and much to do with its fragility and impotence. The ways in which corruption has emerged and developed in parallel with the growth and failures of the African state form the substance of this book.

NOTES

(1)   To acknowledge that corruption is particularly conspicuous in certain contexts does not, in itself, suggest that it is necessarily of great political moment. Clandestine corruption, by definition, commonly escapes public attention, but it often has serious political and economic consequences.

(2)   This study is concerned with political corruption and the analysis of commercial practices is therefore confined to the interaction of business and government.

(3)   This is not to imply that corruption in the United States is trival or inconsequential. Several scholars (Benson, 1978; Berg et.al., 1976; Williams, 1981) have argued that corruption is both more prevalent and more important than is commonly appreciated. The suggestion here is simply that it does not yet pose a threat to political and economic stability.

(4)   Categorisation can be a substitute for, rather than a
        preliminary to, explanation and, where explanatory
        problems are particularly acute, it may be tempting to
        believe that taxonomy constitutes an important step
        towards explanation.

(5)   This is partly a consequence of ethnocentrism and partly a
        question of how far the identification of corruption is
        linked to the observance of formal rules. When
        exceptions become the rule, the status of the formal
        rules requires close examination.

(6)   An early example of the former is (Leff, 1964), while
        (Leys; 1975; Williams (ed.), 1976) are obvious examples of
        Marxist influenced scholarship.

(7)   In the absence of criminal convictions, the possible legal
        consequences make the temptation to name the 'guilty
        men' relatively easy to resist.

(8)   Nigeria's scandals are much publicised and relatively well
        documented, but it should not, of course, be assumed that
        other African states are immune from large-scale
        corruption.

(9)   While there are, obviously, other important constraints, the
        concern here is to emphasis that corruption is not always,
        or even often, perceived as a pressing political priority.

(10)   But it is always possible that the symptoms of corruption
        become so politically distressing that their temporary
        alleviation supercedes the requirements of long-term cure.

2 Understanding political corruption

Corruption, like obscenity, is more readily condemned than defined or explained. The purpose of this chapter is to make a preliminary assessment of what has been said, and what can properly be said, about the study of political corruption. While acknowledging that corruption resists easy measurement and simple interpretation, the chapter attempts to identify some possible sources of confusion and suggests a potentially more fruitful mode of analysis.

The defining of terms can be a tedious and dispiriting task. Defeated by the problem of defining obscenity, Justice Potter Stewart asserted 'I know it when I see it' (quoted in Abraham, 1972, p.180). But such an approach scarcely constitutes a breakthrough in social inquiry because, were it to find general favour, corruption, like obscenity or beauty, could exist only in the eye of the beholder. In such circumstances, the prospects of reaching agreement on the object of study are uncertain and accounts of the character of corruption would be both presumptuous and premature.

The first part of this chapter considers a number of ways of defining corruption and explores the various meanings of the term. This analysis will illuminate the utility of particular definitions and facilitate an appreciation of the role of definition in political inquiry. My purpose is to clear part of the ground and not to try to resolve or pre-empt normative or explanatory problems by definitional means. The attempt to clarify definitional issues is preliminary to, and linked with, a discussion of the ways in which corruption can be analysed and explained. Thus, the second part of this chapter is concerned to evaluate a range of perspectives on political corruption and, in so doing, to set out a justification for the approach employed in this book.

A. Defining Corruption

While dictionaries sometimes offer hope to the anxious student in pursuit of succinct and unambiguous definition, they supply, in the case of corruption, an embarrassment of riches. (1) It seems that corruption has a multiplicity of meanings and the literature demonstrates that different meanings appeal to different scholars. No doubt it is unrealistic to expect a unanimity of approach, but it may prove useful to examine the roles different meanings play in analysing corruption.

In broad terms, dictionary definitions of corruption attribute three basic meanings to the term;

(a) organic or biological corruption
(b) moral corruption
(c) legal or public office corruption.

All three meanings are present in the literature on political corruption and sometimes they appear in the same work. My initial purpose then is to disentangle the different threads of meaning in an effort to make clear their particular place in the study of corruption.

At first sight, the organic or biological sense of corruption appears to possess little utility for, or relevance to, political inquiry. But this is myopic because it seriously underestimates the power and influence of metaphor and analogy in political discourse.   In its organic sense, corruption is popularly invoked to describe and condemn both the decline of states and the more grotesque misbehaviour of politicians and princes.

In the biological sense, the charge of corruption is graphic; to corrupt means to infect, taint, spoil or make putrid by decay or decomposition. Clearly, few polities or politicians would welcome or accept such a description even if some might merit it. Those who compare the conduct of government with the processes of putrefaction deploy an evocative image to convey the strength of their condemnation. Thus, the utility of the organic meaning generally lies less in explaining the nature of corruption, than in underlining or over-emphasising the threat it poses to the survival of the polity in some prescribed form. The organic sense survives not least because it enriches the vocabulary of political invective and abuse.

While the organic meaning is less favoured by contemporary analysts, it still features in accounts which explicitly define corruption in some other way. Spokesmen for public organisations frequently attribute corruption to the odd 'rotten apple' in an otherwise wholesome barrel. (2) It then becomes imperative to remove the putrid fruit before it 'taints' or 'contaminates' the other apples. My concern, at this stage, is not that such analyses are misconceived, nor even to claim that analogies with apples do not reach the core of the problem, but simply to point out that the organic meaning of corruption can, so to speak, contaminate other meanings.

Turning from biology to morality, we find that the dictionary definitions are no less reticent. In moral terms, to corrupt means to pervert, degrade, ruin and debase integrity, virtue or moral principle. Destruction and dissolution are, in the moral sense, to be found in the characters of citizens and rulers and in the consequent decay of moral relations between and among rulers and ruled. In this view, political corruption is a question of moral values and standards and it is the standards we adhere to that will determine whether we deem certain practices to be corrupt.

In the moral realm, an act identified as corrupt is something to be condemned qua corrupt act. Thus, to say that corruption is wrong is rather like saying that murder is wrong. Both statements express what is, in effect, a conceptual truth or grammatical necessity. If either statement were contradicted, it would constitute a proposal for a change in the meaning of corruption or murder.

Corruption is used in this sense to describe a morally repugnant state of political affairs and implicit in its use is the desire to eliminate it (Wraith and Simpkins, 1963).   Thus, analysts who choose to use corruption in its moral sense are interested less in explanation than in condemnation and prescription. To the moralist, sophisticated attempts to locate the possible economic and political benefits of corruption are irrelevant and pointless because the moralist's position cannot be undermined by empirical investigation. Moral standards are applied to, rather than emerge from, particular situations. They are external, not intrinsic, to disputes about the nature of corruption. This is especially clear with religious or ideological accounts which affirm specific standards as the only acceptable and correct ones.

Implicit in the moral meaning of corruption is the judgement that a corrupt society perverts or destroys the potential for a moral and civilised existence. What, in principle, would a morally corrupt society look like? According to some accounts (Dobel,

1978), the morally corrupt society is one where moral life has, so to speak, been privatised. As a result, social relations are characterised by complete self-interest and fellow citizens are seen as instruments, obstacles and competitors. In the morally corrupt society, civic virtue and social responsibility are abandoned and intense competition for spoils becomes the dominant social mode.

Unless and until integrity, virtue and moral principle are re-asserted, political life is limited to an unseemly and unceasing scramble for the fruits of public office. In such circumstances, dire political consequences are inescapable and it becomes increasingly difficult to resist the disintegration of legal and governmental processes. Such disintegration is accompanied and accelerated by a decline in political loyalty and co-operation and a sharply increasing tendency to instability and violence. (3)

In the corrupt polity, power depends on efficient coercion and effective bribery, on suppressing sporadic uprisings and co-opting potential opponents. These techniques for maintaining political mastery are as well understood in parts of modern Africa as they were in fifteenth century Florence.

Moral indignation at corruption seems to derive partly from the fear that, once it has taken hold, corruption is almost impossible to eliminate. To express the strength of their conviction, moralists are prone to employ the language of organic decay and violation. Corruption may be likened to cancer in order to convey the gravity of the situation and the often inexorable spread of the disease (Hodder-Williams, 1984, p.111). More luridly, the corrupt can be depicted as vampires or leeches draining virtuous blood from the body politic. Whatever the image, moralists agree that the prognosis is poor when the condition is well advanced. The grounds for pessimism are clear in that moral outrage lacks both outlet and audience in the corrupt society. What was once regarded as morally degenerate is accepted as conventional behaviour and occasional deviance becomes standard practice.

Although moral evaluation uses a general set of standards to condemn corrupt behaviour, it does not offer a means of identifying and explaining specific instances of corruption in different societies. It does not admit the possibility that what is meant by corruption may vary from society to society and nor does it take any account of the perceptions of participants. Where moral standards conflict, there is no independent means of reconciling them or deciding which should prevail.

Modern social scientists have, for the most part, eschewed the value laden approach of the moralist. They prefer to refine and adapt the legal or public office meaning of corruption in the hope that this meaning offers an escape both from moralism and the pungent vocabulary of the pathology laboratory.

> Webster's defines corruption as; 'inducement (as of a political official) by means of improper considerations (as bribery) to commit a violation of duty'. The selling of political favours or other improper political or legal transactions or arrangements.

The Oxford definitions are broadly similar, but with stronger echoes of other meanings. In the Oxford version, the transitive verb corrupt means;

> 'to destroy or pervert the integrity or fidelity of (a person) in his discharge of duty; to induce to act dishonestly or unfaithfully;to make venal; to bribe'.

It is useful to note the specificity and inclusiveness of the above definitions. They explicitly include bribery and encompass both the giving and receiving of bribes. They focus on corruption as a particular form of disloyalty and as a breach of faith or trust. But they are less specific about embezzlement and other forms of what is sometimes called auto-corruption. In these dictionary definitions, the essence of corruption is located in some form of illicit, illegal or otherwise improper transaction or relationship between someone performing a public duty and someone seeking undue and unwarranted preference or advantage.

The overlap in the organic and moral uses of the term corruption is paralleled by the legal and moral uses in that the perversion or destruction of integrity is crucial to both the legal and moral meanings. But the legal sense is to be distinguished by its emphasis on the improper discharge of public duties. Whatever the precise meaning of 'improper', it inevitably embraces conduct which violates specific rules governing the way public duties should be performed.

If the moral sense of corruption appeals to standards or values, the legal meaning appeals to rules and laws. It relates corruption to the violation of a rule and that notion is correspondingly related to a particular motive, improper advantage or gain. Legal judgements supply one sort of answer to the question, what is corruption? But the answer is a strictly limited one because legal judgements only apply in the context of the administration of justice to people who are already, prima facie, thought to have contravened rules or laws prohibiting corrupt behaviour.

Legal adjudication relates acts to rules in ways intended to reveal the contravention of specific rules by particular acts. It is concerned with whether acts are in compliance with, or in contravention of, rules and the terms 'guilt' and 'innocence' precisely state the occurrence or non-occurrence of compliance. In the legal judgement, as in the moral evaluation, no reference is made to the actor's conception of the significance of his actions. A defendant's refusal to recognise a court or be bound by its rules may have political or ideological significance but, unless he can appeal to some legal principle or procedural impropriety, his claims are irrelevant to the process of legal adjudication.

The upsurge of academic interest in political corruption in the 1960s produced a spate of new definitions. For the most part, these definitions were 'new' in the sense used by purveyors of detergents. They consisted largely in elaborations or re-formulations of the legal/public office meaning which was thought to be more compatible with the goal of a value-free social science. Thus the legal/public office meaning was stretched and strained as analysts sought to formulate a definition which was simultaneously general enough to permit comparative study and yet specific enough to justify making valid observations on particular countries. The early appreciation that laws vary from country to country discouraged a purely legal emphasis and ensured that increasing reference was made to public office definitions.

Despite strenuous efforts, it has proved difficult to improve on the public office definition offered by J.S. Nye (1967, p. 419). Nye's definition is widely cited in modern studies and it contains a succinct, yet comprehensive, account of the public office sense of the term. According to Nye, corruption is;

> behaviour which deviates from the formal duties of a public role because of private-regarding (personal, close family, private clique) pecuniary or status gains; or violates rules against the exercise of certain types of private-regarding influence. This includes such behaviour as bribery (use of a reward to pervert the judgement of a person in a position of trust); nepotism (bestowal of patronage by reason of ascriptive relationship rather than merit); and misappropriation (illegal appropriation of public resources for private-regarding uses).

Although the above definition seems capacious, it contains no a priori assumptions about the consequences of corruption and it does not address the question of whether behaviour defined as corrupt is perceived as corrupt in any particular society. It is an explicitly public office definition in that it is concerned with deviation from rules and formal duties rather than with moral or physical decay and it clearly identifies bribery, nepotism and misappropriation as the main types of corrupt behaviour.

But Nye's definition requires some clarification because, despite its apparent precision, it contains several possible ambiguities. First, the term 'behaviour' embraces not only improper action in the performance of public duties, but also inaction, the wilful failure to act when required to do so. Corruption frequently involves attempts to induce officials not to enforce particular laws or regulations.

More significantly, Nye's definition excludes the activities of powerful lobbyists and interest groups unless they seek to accomplish their ends through bribery or otherwise violate rules governing the discharge of public duties. Similarly, a government which systematically favours a particular ethnic group or region in the distribution of public resources need not, in Nye's terms, be corrupt. His definition is indifferent to the fairness or otherwise of the ends and priorities of governments, rather it addresses itself to the conduct of politicians and officials and to the means they employ in discharging their public duties.

There is no doubt that legal/public office definitions of political corruption have considerable merit. Laws and rules not only offer some hope of precision and consistency, but they are regularly subject to judicial interpretation and refinement. Evolving judicial standards are often adopted by the police and other law-enforcement agencies and applied to actual cases. Thus, the legal definition recommends itself to many scholars both because the illegality of behaviour is part of contemporary notions of corruption and because the legal environment has an effect on the nature, scope and consequence of such behaviour.

But, despite their attractions, it is also clear that legal/public office definitions have important limitations and inadequacies. In Britain, general acceptance of the notion that citizens are, or ought to be, considered equal before the law, and therefore merit equal treatment, lends credence to the belief that the law is somehow neutral or impartial and free from partisan, class, sexual or ethnic bias. Such assumptions are, of course, open to serious question. Laws are not made by angels and it may be more useful to see the legislative process as an arena for political competition and conflict in which the winners translate their victories into general rules binding on their political opponents.

When the law is treated as anything other than a political product, it is hard to resist attributing some normative value to whatever legal standards of official conduct happen to prevail. In this regard, it is important to remember that it is often possible for the politically powerful to legitimate their conduct by manipulating legislative and legal processes. The law is not static and, in any society, legal definitions of what constitutes corruption 'are a function of ideological and power considerations which are constantly changing'. (Szeftel in Clarke (ed) 1983, p.186) As laws change, conduct that was once legal may be deemed corrupt and behaviour that used to be illegal may become legitimate.

Similarly, since laws vary from society to society, behaviour which is legitimate in country X may be corrupt in country Y. A gift from a building contractor to a housing minister may, depending on the country, be categorised as a legitimate campaign contribution or as a bribe. If the rules governing the financing of elections are tightly drawn, one consequence for Africa is that political parties and organisations which are not funded by the state find it difficult to raise adequate funds by legitimate means.

Thus, although legality is a very important factor in understanding corruption, other perspectives and considerations may be of equal significance. If legality is determined by the politically powerful, it may be tempting to conclude that to employ legal criteria for identifying corrupt behaviour is to endorse the authority of the strong rather than the just. Those who reach such conclusions are more likely to define corruption in terms of abstractions such as the common good or the public interest and to describe it in terms of the subversion of the public interest for private ends. In particular cases, the common good may be regarded as synonymous with the creation or maintenance of a specific set of political arrangments and corruption identified as behaviour likely to undermine such arrangements.

Corruption may be spoken of as inimical to the public interest, but it is not always clear whether this is the case. We do not possess a consensus on what constitutes the public interest and, until we do, we lack criteria for determining whether certain forms of conduct undermine it. The public interest is likely to remain an elusive, amorphous concept which will always be susceptible to conflicting interpretation by competing interests in society. Special interest groups will no doubt continue to claim that their objectives are in the public interest, but we lack any agreed means of reconciling or resolving such conflicting claims.

If legality can serve as an instrument of the politically powerful, the notion of the public interest can be equally useful. Just as ruling groups can manipulate legislative and legal processes, so can they represent their private benefits to be in the common, national or public interest. It therefore seems difficult to resist the conclusion that the public interest approach to corruption amounts to 'an attempt to solve an essentially normative or ideological question by definition'. (Scott, 1972, p.3)

Given that legality and the public interest are prone to

appropriation by the politically powerful, an alternative method of identifying corruption is to use public opinion as the relevant standard for assessing conduct. At first glance, such an approach seems attractive, not least because there is little doubt that public opinion plays an influential role both in stimulating governmental responses to corruption and in determining the effectiveness of anti-corruption measures.

But public opinion is not monolithic. It often proves divided, unstable, ambiguous and inconsistent, even assuming that accurate measurement is possible (Peil, 1974). What we sweepingly term public opinion is, in effect, the opinions of many different and often competing 'publics'.

Not only is the character of the 'public' in question, but the use of public opinion as a measure of corruption also raises some comparative difficulties. Public opinion changes over time and what is corrupt today may be regarded as legitimate tomorrow. Public opinion tends to vary from country to country, from region to region and perhaps from city to countryside. Even if a stable consensus on what constituted corruption were to emerge in any particular society, it is clear both that some opinions count more than others and that intensity of feeling can outweigh the apathy of majorities. Political and economic position, physical location and popular anger are all crucial factors in assessing the influence of public opinion. Quantitative measures alone are inadequate because, as the proverb nearly said, never mind the width, feel the quality of opinion.

Having sought to clarify the ways in which political corruption has most frequently been defined, it is necessary, if slightly invidious, to suggest that the importance of defining the term has perhaps been either misunderstood or exaggerated. One possible source of difficulty lies in the apparent presumption that a specific and irrevocable choice needs to be made about which meaning of corruption to employ. Yet no all-purpose definition is available. How corruption is defined is partly a function of the kinds of questions analysts pose and what it is they wish to understand. It is, of course, important to be clear about what we mean, but it is not compulsory, and may not be desirable, to adhere rigidly to only one meaning. What is more important is that we are clear about which meaning is being used at any particular point in our analysis.

The choice of definition is intimately related to the direction in which we wish our analysis to go, but our choice need not exclude consideration of aspects of corruption central to other definitions. If, for example, we define corruption in legal/public office terms, we are not precluded from examining how such corruption is regarded by public opinion nor from inquiring into its consequences for the population at large. Similarly, if we define corruption in terms of popular attitudes, we may still wish to investigate the possible incongruence of attitudes with legal norms and to assess the influence of the legal framework on the climate of public opinion.

There is clearly a close affinity between the public interest and moralist definitions of corruption in that both are concerned less with corruption, than with the damage it does to society. Nevertheless, if we assume that corruption is 'bad', we may still wish to inquire into its persistence. Conceivably, our analysis could prompt us to consider why laws against corruption are not enforced, why public opinion does not unanimously condemn it, and why efforts to combat corruption are often less than successful.

More importantly, we need to accord definitions their proper place in social inquiry. Definitions are neither explanations nor statements of indisputable fact. They are more like proposals, to be accepted or rejected, or like rules, to be complied with or violated. By exaggerating the problems of definition, it is possible to mistake definitional molehills for explanatory mountains. Students of corruption should remember that 'definitions are only conventions and apply only because of agreement that they should apply'. (Ryan, 1971, p.5) Definitions, like conventions, can be questioned, modified and replaced when they are no longer acceptable.

The defining of terms is, or ought to be, a preliminary to, not a substitute for, explanation and definitions should be aids not obstacles to understanding corruption. However defined, corruption is a feature of political life which demands awareness of, and sensitivity to, a variety of perspectives. Such an awareness reduces the danger of tunnel vision and may help in providing a richer and fuller account of the place of corruption in African politics.

It will be argued that corruption resists simple definition because it is not a discrete phenomenon, separate and distinct from all other forms of political and administrative behaviour. Thus, despite the important analytical merits of the legal/public office definition, legal corruption frequently forms only part of a broader pattern or style of political behaviour in Africa. Corruption cannot be properly understood if it is isolated and abstracted from the context in which it occurs. To understand fully the role of corruption in African settings, it will therefore be necessary to go beyond the confines of the formal legal framework.

B. Explaining Corruption

This section offers a preliminary sketch of a number of ways of explaining corruption. Some explanations form part of major theoretical enterprises and it is beyond the scope of this study to accord them extended consideration. My present purpose is only to indicate the explanatory directions taken by recent studies and to note their most striking features. The issues raised in this provisional discussion will be further addressed in the chapters to follow.

Corruption in Africa can be defined and explained in a variety of incompatible ways. But, in some cases, the explanation amounts to little more than an elaboration of the initial definition. Thus, to define corruption in moral terms solves, in one sense, the problem of explaining it. Avarice and greed are central to the moralist account and human weaknesses, rather than political and economic factors, are identified as both the source of corruption and the proper object of remedial attention. (Benson, 1978, pp. 273-295)

If low moral standards cause corruption, higher ones will cure it. Thus, the moralists' prescription involves recruiting and training 'incorruptible' public servants. But moral fibre is hard to detect and harder to instill. Those susceptible to corruption are rarely equipped with horns and this makes their early identification problematic.

Moralists explain corruption in terms of individual lapses from specified standards of official conduct, but problems arise when members of the same society operate according to different and conflicting codes of behaviour. If to adhere to one code is to violate another, which should prevail? In making such judgements, the moralist is forced to assert the superiority, even the universality, of his own moral values. In certain cases, Western observers recognise only Western standards of conduct as modern, progressive or universal. Alternative patterns of loyalty and responsibility may be described as 'primordial' or anachronistic.

As the charge of 'cultural imperialism' grew harder to ignore, students of political corruption searched for an explanatory framework which would both avoid ethnocentrism and facilitate comparative analysis. The quest was a difficult one, but some located the Holy Grail in functionalist theory. Functionalism is, of course, much more than an explanation of corruption in that it purports to offer a general theory of society. It came into social science from biology and, recalling the earlier discussion of the organic sense of the term, it is not surprising that it should appeal to some students of corruption.

The first claims for functionalism in social science were made by social anthropologists in the 1920s. But while it is clear that there were, and are, varieties of functional analysis, it is equally clear that the different forms share a common perspective. In studying a given social or political system, the functionalist asks 'not how a pattern of behaviour may have originated so much as what part it plays in maintaining the system as a whole' (Runciman, 1969, p.110).

Thus, instead of pre-judging and prescribing, functionalists seek to explain recurrent social behaviour as fulfilling, or contributing to, specific societal needs. As an enduring and prominent feature of political activity in Africa, corruption is assumed to perform some essential political functions. Far from undermining good government and destroying social relations, corruption may be seen as helping to maintain political stability and social integration.

But it is often not at all clear what the term 'function' means and, when it is closely linked to the notion of a 'political system', there is more than a suggestion of tautology. Gabriel Almond's formulation of structural-functionalism in The Politics of the Developing Areas (1960) not only assumes that the term 'system' is unobjectionable, but fails to define the key concept of 'function'.

To demonstrate that a particular pattern of political behaviour has important social consequences may be useful and interesting, but it does not explain the behaviour. Corruption may or may not contribute to stability, growth and harmony in Africa, but the alleged functionality requires proof not simple assertion. While demonstrating that corruption has 'useful' consequences is problematic, it would still not explain how it originated or why it takes the form it does.

In the 1960s, functionalism appeared to many scholars to offer a major leap forward in political science. It was, or seemed to be, value-free and it promised to make a science of comparative politics possible. (4) But Gabriel Almond's ambition to build a theory of political development remains unfulfilled. The logical problems of functional analysis and systems theory are formidable (5) and what Almond offers is less a theory of political behaviour, than a terminology within which theories may be constructed. The lesson for the student of corruption is perhaps that it is better to travel slowly on foot than to join a theoretical flight which regularly crashes on take-off.

We have seen, thus far, that moralism and functionalism both seek to place corruption in a wider framework. On closer examination, we can see that these frameworks are mutually exclusive. Corruption is depicted either as a manifestation of human weakness or, conversely, as evidence of human persistence and ingenuity in overcoming adversity. Where the moralist sees only deficiencies in individual consciences, the functionalist focuses on the limitations of formal institutions and procedures. In both cases, the result is corruption. For the moralist, the undermining of integrity produces the dissolution of the polity; for the functionalist, integrating the polity often requires the undermining of integrity.

It was suggested earlier that it is a mistake to abstract corruption from the political context in which it occurs. Such an abstraction could imply that explanations of corruption are independent of, or indifferent to, wider disputes about the character of African politics. But vigorous theoretical and historical disputes continue to flourish because Almond's anticipated revolution in political science qua science seems to have been indefinitely postponed. The sharp divisions concerning what might loosely be termed development theory inhibit, or possibly even preclude, the emergence of a consensus on political corruption and many other key issues.

Disputes about the causes or character of corruption in Africa are, in practice, intimately connected to wider debates about development, dependency and the nature of the post-colonial state. Explanations of corruption should therefore be located with an appropriate frame of reference. But, in a short book, it is hardly possible to do adequate justice to the rigorous and vigorous debates which have so dominated the study of African politics in the past twenty five years. My purpose here is limited to the task of indicating how contending interpretations of African politics have shaped and structured explanations of political corruption.

Given that the goal of bringing the jungle of African studies to a state of orderly cultivation is far beyond the scope and ambition of this study, there remains a need for a provisional guide to the flora and fauna. Although the problems of classification are formidable, the approach adopted here assumes, for simplicity's sake, that there are two main schools of thought, the 'nationalist' and the 'internationalist'. (Clapham, 1985, p.6) No one would seriously deny that there are important disputes within these schools but, for present purposes, the above labels conveniently convey what seems to be a fundamental difference in approach.

The internationalist approach places great emphasis on the power of economic forces to shape, or even determine, both the nature of the state and the distribution of political benefits. The organising concept is 'underdevelopment' and analysis focuses on the global development of capitalism and its impact on Africa. In this view, the economic structures and political arrangements of underdeveloped states in Africa are only explicable in terms of their incorporation into an international economic system.

In one version, dependency theory, a view is presented of ruling groups in Africa which reduces them to the status of 'agents of foreign domination'. (Higgott, 1983, p.66) Dependency theory sees the post-colonial state as the protector and guardian of foreign economic interests and as a vital link in the chain connecting international with local capital. In conditions of economic dependence, political independence is deemed illusory and military and civilian rulers alike are judged prisoners of circumstance rather than masters of their own destinies. Unless and until the chains of international capitalism are loosened or severed, political independence will remain more rhetorical than real.

While dependency theory is pre-occupied by international trade and the unequal terms on which it is conducted, Marxist oriented theory focuses on the modes of production prevalent in dependent capitalist economies and on the social formations they generate. To the Marxist, the processes of production are the key to class formation and the appropriation of economic surpluses. But whether the concern is with circulation and exchange relationships or with control of the means of production, the internationalist approach clearly depicts Africa's ruling groups as dependent, parasitic and coercive.

The notion of underdevelopment suggests that African economies are locked into the production of primary products and the implication is that state revenues are largely dependent on the regulation of trade. This task therefore becomes the first concern of government and, in the process, politics and administration take on a new character. The 'neo-mercantalist' state is born and the internationalist perspective perceives the post-colonial state in Africa as more and more like 'an import-export agency' (Dunn, 1978, p.15)

If African governments are peceived as intimately connected to, and constrained by, international capitalism, it comes as no surprise when corruption is explained as a product or consequence of such intimacy. When internal markets are small, external trade offers the major opportunity for acquiring wealth and foreign exchange. Those responsible for the regulation of such commerce, 'the mercantile administocracy' (Crook in Lyon and Manor (eds), 1983, p.187) are, of course, strategically placed to enrich themselves. Thus, to the internationalist, large-scale corruption is attributed to the activities of the comprador bourgeoisie who both collaborate with multi-national companies and other vehicles of international capitalism and who have access to local political power and the fruits of public office.

The internationalist perspective clearly accords primacy to

structural economic factors. The nature of the economy in an underdeveloped country and the place of that economy in the international economic system are both assigned a major part in determining the character of political and administrative activity. But the nationalist approach rejects this as deterministic and argues that there are numerous anomalies which invalidate the theoretical claims of dependency and other internationalist approaches.

The nationalist perspective focuses on the internal evolution of states rather than on their external manipulation. (6) But the early contributions from this school frequently used general organising concepts like development and modernisation to facilitate comparative analysis. Insofar as political change was explained in terms of stages of development, corruption was described, like adolescence, as a phase, a transitional condition which would pass. Thus, the sometimes distressing symptoms of corruption were diagnosed as growing pains rather than as malignant disease. The industrial societies of Western Europe and North America were thought to have passed from a corrupt condition to a more or less pure one and it was thought that the countries of the Third World would prove susceptible to a similar cleansing process.

The notions of development and modernisation have been subject to fierce criticism and it could generally be agreed that the approach has proved less fruitful than its pioneers once hoped. The disappointments of development theory had a chastening effect and the theoretical claims of the nationalist school became more circumspect and muted. Studies became more detailed and their conclusions less sweeping. Explanations of corruption seemed to require particular attention to specific circumstances rather than a small slot in a general evolutionary theory. Small became beautiful and micro analysis supplanted macro theory.

While the limitations of development theory became increasingly apparent, the nationalist school continued to reject the claims of the underdevelopment or internationalist school. Their unit of analysis was the African state and not the international economic order. Thus the nationalist school argues for the primacy of politics over economics. It elevates political and administrative choice above the constraints of economic circumstance. By so doing, it asserts the significance of the internal against the international and emphasises the contingent against the systemic. Such a perspective directs attention to the variables within the political system and, in particular, it focuses on the structure of local political competition and on the arrangements and procedures which provide opportunities for corruption. Within such a framework, it is also possible to adduce cultural, psychological and sociological considerations in explaining the incidence of corruption.   To the extent that an external dimension to corruption is recognised, it is as an additional factor rather than as the major cause.

Despite the obvious inadequacies of my cursory treatment of the nationalist and internationalist perspectives, (7) there should be no doubt that explanations of corruption form part of wider interpretations of African and Third World politics.   Such interpretations are themselves connected to general arguments about the nature and interaction of political, economic, and social change.   Thus, to understand particular accounts of corruption, it is important to expose the fundamental assumptions on which the accounts are based.

To argue, for example, that corruption arises because governments disrupt or distort market forces in allocating resources is to assume that market forces are inexorable.   To suggest the dismantling of the regulatory apparatus of the state as a cure for corruption is to assume that the consequences of such action are bound to be, in some sense, more acceptable than the prevailing level of corruption.   By definition, the less government there is, the fewer the opportunities there are for political and administrative misconduct.   But eliminating the regulatory activity of the state is both inherently improbable and likely to produce other and possibly less attractive consequences than restricting opportunities for corruption. Reducing the level of corruption is not, and could not be, the only important objective of African governments. In practice, it may not be an objective at all.

If corruption is assumed to be a consequence of the character of political regimes in Africa, the problem becomes one of explaining the nature of the modern African state.   It is, in effect, to substitute one set of explanatory problems for another.   To describe the African state as 'neo-mercantalist' or to depict official conduct as 'neo-patrimonial' (Clapham, 1985, pp. 44-51) is to broaden and perhaps to simplify the issue.   No doubt once the conceptual framework is firmly established, corruption can be placed in its appropriate slot.   But the problem remains of determining which framework explains what kinds of corruption.

Whether corruption is explained in terms of development or underdevelopment, morality or Marxism, market forces or mercantalism, functionalism or class formation, the lesson is simple and clear.   Different assumptions, perspectives and values produce differing accounts.   While economic determinism and political voluntarism have their contending champions,, the student of corruption is not required to choose sides before, or even perhaps after, examining what the different sides identify as evidence.

It is possible that the modern states of Africa resist simple or complex categorisation. It may also be conceded that the variety of circumstance and experience preclude the acceptance of any general explanation of political corruption in Africa. Given the physical, political, historical and economic disparities of, for example, Zimbabwe and Zaire or Kenya and Nigeria, it would be remarkable if the origins, incidence and structure of corruption in such dissimilar societies are susceptible to any single general explanation.

C. Problems and Prospects

Whatever the approach adopted, political corruption is likely to remain a peculiarly difficult subject to study. Corruption is often clandestine and the topic is always politically sensitive. The quest for reliable information about corruption is a journey beset by obstacles and hazards that often yields only uncertain rewards. The available data is soft, not hard, and the numerate political scientist finds few reliable numbers to 'crunch'. This deficiency may help account for the relative, but conspicuous, neglect of corruption in the work of some distinguished American specialists in the field of political development. (8)

The study of political corruption in Africa poses particularly acute problems because official statistics and the accounts of public bodies are, to say the least, not always available, reliable or up-to-date. In extreme cases, what passes for financial information is entirely the product of bureaucratic imagination. It seems unlikely that the capacity and willingness to produce more accurate accounts will develop in the foreseeable future.

But research problems extend beyond the realm of official statistics. Access to senior civil servants, government ministers and military rulers is difficult and, self-incrimination aside, it is hard to evaluate official responses to inquiries about corruption. Unsurprisingly, those in receipt of improper favours or otherwise involved in the bribe process rarely clamour to participate in political science surveys of corruption. This is not to say that there is little to be gleaned from surveys of public attitudes to corruption, but rather to emphasise that both survey conditions and the nature of the subject ensure that their findings require careful handling.

It is not only extremely difficult to measure the incidence of corruption, but it is even more difficult to assess its importance. It is frequently cited as responsible for all manner of political discontents and it is almost invariably used by soldiers to justify their seizure of power. Allegations of corruption may be used by those in power to eliminate troublesome rivals and by those in opposition to discredit the government. Where accusations of corruption serve as a prime political tactic, there may well be smoke without fire. Conversely, when leading members of a regime are brought to trial, it should not be assumed that the other members of the government are pure and untainted. Corruption is part of the political process and attempts to measure or evaluate it must recognise this central feature.

Corruption is not, of course, a monolithic phenomenon. It comes in many forms and operates at different levels. It may be trivial and incidental or serious and systematic. It can touch nearly all the members of a society or be confined to a limited group. Explanations of corruption enjoy a similar diversity and may focus on individuals, on institutions, on political systems or even on global economic forces. Corruption may be seen as functional or dysfunctional, as something to be condoned or condemned. It may be accorded a central explanatory role in interpreting the character of African politics or dismissed as a by-product, a consequence of more important factors. In assessing the validity of competing perspectives and judgements on corruption, we are seriously short of compelling evidence. To ask whether corruption is a cause or a result of political and economic change is to pose a deceptively simple question which has no obvious or unambiguous answer.

If corruption is clandestine and there are no accurate financial records, the task of appraising the scale and economic impact of corruption is formidable. It seems, therefore, almost inevitable that the 'evidence' used by students of corruption is bound to be fragmentary, biased, anecdotal, potentially misleading, impressionistic and inadequate. We must do the best we can with the materials to hand but, clearly, only a reckless builder would construct an explanatory castle on such flimsy and uncertain foundations. The study of political corruption in Africa thus encourages a proper sense of humility and modesty, qualities not always prominent in political science. This book does not therefore offer a new general theory of corruption nor even a significant move 'toward' one. Until someone produces a general theory, we are not able to say whether the ideas and insights in this and other works have helped or hindered in the task.

To admit that the research 'evidence' is, in many respects, unsatisfactory is not to say that political corruption is less important, less worthy of study than more accessible and measurable aspects of African politics. Neither does such an admission entail accepting that little can be said about the origins, incidence, anatomy and control of political corruption. What it does entail is that generalisations should be treated as tentative, provisional and qualified. The 'laws' of corruption will probably continue to elude us, but political scientists have long since learned to live with such disappointments. While our aims are modest, we should acknowledge that, in principle, statements about corruption are of similar status to those made about other political phenomena. It may well be possible to discern trends and patterns of corrupt behaviour, to discover key variables and significant linkages and to detect crucial economic and political conditions without being able to translate such findings into mathematical propositions or scientific theories.

Understanding corruption in Africa involves not only rejecting a premature commitment to any one conceptual framework, but it also requires sensitivity to the contribution of a number of academic disciplines. It requires an awareness of the limited utility of the public office definition and a willingness to consider competing perspectives. It means avoiding making assumptions about the functionality or otherwise of corruption in advance of, or in the absence of, any substantial and reliable evidence. Where the evidence is inadequate or unreliable, it demands that we resist the temptation to impose order and coherence on what may actually be chaos and confusion.

To enhance the prospects of acquiring a proper understanding of corruption, it is necessary to pose a number of specific questions. We have to ask how corruption developed and identify the factors that contributed to its growth. We need to know what forms it takes and examine why particular types are more prevalent than others. It is also clearly important to grasp whether certain kinds of political system are prone to produce and sustain high levels of corruption or whether each case is unique. Finally, we have to ask what obstacles there are to containing or reducing corruption in modern Africa. The following chapters address these questions and attempt to produce some tentative, incomplete and uncertain answers. The aim is to provide some useful points of illumination rather than to disperse the fog. Corruption remains an intractable subject which exposes, in an acute form, the explanatory limitations of modern social science.

To accept the limitations of our inquiry is not to concede that our understanding must continue to be shaped by the inadequacies of prevailing conceptual frameworks. While corruption is conventionally depicted as infractions of the rules of political conduct, understanding the significance of such infringements requires not just a grasp of the rules but some insight into the nature of the political game. The next chapter examines the origins of the game in Africa and outlines the significance of, and reaction to, the imposition of new rules of conduct.

NOTES

(1)   The dictionary definitions analysed in this study are taken from the Oxford English Dictionary and Webster's Third New International Dictionary.

(2)   Other responses may involve recognising the need for major reforms, but the purging of individuals serves to distract attention from more general issues. The characteristic British response to corruption has been well documented (Doig, 1984).

(3)   Elements of this description are clearly present in many African states and, in the case of Zaire, it has been argued that the entire system is corrupt (Gould, 1980).

(4)   For a sophisticated and amusing discussion of the scale of the task, see Alasdair MacIntyre's essay, 'Is a Science of Comparative Politics Possible?' (MacIntyre, 1971).

(5)   The critical literature is extensive, but perhaps the most accessible are (Beattie, 1964; Runciman, 1969; and Ryan, 1971).

(6)   By discounting or ignoring external manipulation, it is possible to write a major work on the problem of maintaining political stability in the Third World (Huntington, 1968) and yet make only one reference to the activities of the Central Intelligence Agency.

(7)   The literature is considerable and often daunting, but (Roxborough, 1978; and Higgott, 1983) are accessible and perceptive introductions to the field.

(8)   More provocatively, it has been suggested that, to Washington policymakers and real politik scholars corruption is an acceptable price to pay to avert the radical political alternatives of Cuba and Nicaragua (Whitehead in Clarke (ed), 1983, p. 159).

3 The genesis of corruption

This chapter explores a variety of factors and circumstances which encouraged the growth of political corruption in Africa. It focuses, in particular, on a combination of social, political and economic changes which have helped to produce enviroments conducive to corruption. The point is not merely that corruption evolves within particular contexts, but also that the environmental matrices which generate corruption are themselves subject to change. Thus, the structure and scale of corruption in Africa is not fixed or immutable, but rather reflects the pressures, constraints, opportunities and incentives which prevail at any particular moment in time.

Historical scholarship and academic reputations thrive on controversy. Long established stereotypes and other expressions of conventional wisdom are grist to the mill of those seeking to establish or confirm alternative interpretations. The study of African history is, of course, no exception and the familiar stereotypes of pre-colonial Africa (1) have increasingly been challenged and criticised. Historical controversy has its sociological counterpart and, in particular, the traditional/modern dichotomy has fallen out of favour. (2) The resolution of such controversies both exceeds the scope of this book and the competence of its author, but we should be careful to ensure that the fires of criticism are not confined to the destruction of straw men. It seems highly improbable, for example, that any contemporary student of African history or politics would use the term, 'traditional society', to suggest that only form of social organisation or one set of attitudes or values prevailed in the pre-colonial era. Terms like 'traditional' may have acquired a dubious reputation, but the question remains as to how to characterise the impact of the European powers and how to emphasise the discontinuities with the pre-colonial era (Hodder-Williams, 1984, pp 11-18).

Given the obvious diversity of peoples and practices in Africa, generalisation can damage both academic health and reputation. It therefore seems incumbent on those who seek to characterise the pre-colonial, colonial or post-independence phases of African history to surround their analyses with qualifying and conditional phrases. But, in a forest of qualification, it is easy not to see the wood for the trees and therefore the account which follows is perhaps less sensitive to anomalies and exceptions than the evidence justifies.

An initial difficulty in analysing corruption in pre-colonial Africa is that the criteria discussed in the preceding chapter appear to have only limited relevance to many of the prevalent forms of social organisation. While conflicts between individuals or between groups were sometimes arbitrated and regulated by a common authority in pre-colonial Africa, it is not reasonable to assume that such authorities were direct equivalents of what we now call governments. 'Traditional' authorities are not synonymous with modern bureaucracies and the significance of their respective roles is conditioned by the particular contexts in which they occur.

Although 'chiefs' and other rulers may have assumed or acquired responsibilities for raising taxes or armies, they also often performed a variety of other functions which, in 'modern' societies, have become the province of specialised, separate non-governmental institutions. The point is not only that such rulers fulfilled what we now regard as social, economic and judicial functions, as well as governmental, but rather that there was often no clear distinction between these roles nor any conception of a conflict of interest in performing them.

In such contexts, sharp or rigid distinctions between private and public or family and work which are familiar to societies where the bureaucratic ethos has become established seem inappropriate and misconceived. Public office definitions of corruption assume an acceptance of bureaucratic values and are therefore of little utility when applied to non-bureaucratic societies. If there is no entity recognisable as a government or bureaucracy, it is difficult to see how one can speak of political corruption. If such entities were frequently absent in pre-colonial Africa, there were exceptions and, for example, bureaucratic forms had developed in Northern Nigeria before the spread of colonialism (Smith, 1964).

Despite such exceptions, it remains the case that, without a perception of some demarcation between discharging public responsibilities and furthering private interests, assertions about the incidence of corruption are problematic. To labour the point, it is difficult to see how an absolute monarch can be corrupt when, by definition, there is no accepted distinction between the man and office, between what is personal and what is public. Without such distinctions, there are no obvious criteria for determining what constitutes improper conduct. (3)

Where bureaucratic forms had emerged, there were nonetheless countervailing factors which discouraged or impeded the spread of corrupt practices. Modern governments have extensive and diverse impacts on their societies but, in 'traditional' Africa, the scope for corruption was generally limited to the manipulation of elections for 'chief' and to improper influence in the arbitration of disputes. If the scope for corruption was so restricted, it seems likely that the incidence of corruption was low.

The money economy was by no means pervasive in pre-colonial Africa and this probably inhibited the growth of corruption. Not only is there likely to be less need for corruption in a subsistence economy, but the means of bribery are harder to acquire and illicit transactions are therefore more difficult to organise and complete. If money, salt or other easily negotiable commodities facilitate corrupt transactions, the availability of luxuries on which to spend illicit gains presumably also acts as a powerful incentive. Where societies lack such goods and there are few outlets for wealth, the incentive for corruption is correspondingly diminished. It therefore seems unlikely that what we now call corruption was a prominent feature of pre-colonial African societies not least because they often lacked the appropriate resources, values, incentives and opportunities.

A. Colonialism and Corruption

The colonial phase of African history gave rise to major changes which had far reaching consequences for the nature and extent of corruption. It is, on occasion, temptingly convenient to attribute every undesirable feature of modern African life to the pernicious legacy of colonial rule. It can be blamed for economic underdevelopment, political instability, 'tribalism' and, of course, for corruption. Although African leaders have sometimes found it convenient to use colonialism as a useful scapegoat in deflecting responsibility for their countries' ills, it does not necessarily mean that such charges are without foundation. However one draws up a balance sheet for the consequences of colonial rule (4), it can scarcely be denied that it disrupted the functioning of African societies. The form and scale of disruption were subject to considerable variation but, even where the hand of colonial rule was lightest, the consequences were often considerable.

Just as 'traditional' societies varied enormously, so did their responses to imperial expansion and colonial rule. (5) The variations were influenced by a number of factors including the character of the colonising state, its motives for expansion, conquest or settlement and the nature of the political and social entities which the colonisers encountered. For present purposes, it is necessary to simplify what were highly complex sets of interactions, but while simplification obviously entails omission, it need not produce gross distortion. The concern here is to identify only those themes and tendencies that can be seen to have influenced the growth of corruption.

Until almost the end of the nineteenth century, the African interior was virtually untouched by the forces of imperial expansion. European contact was more commercial than political and conquest was limited mainly to a number of ports and coastal settlements. The principal aim was to facilitate and control trade and, if such aims could be achieved by informal, inexpensive means, then so much the better. Ultimately, imperial expansion was backed by force, but that did not mean that other methods were readily forsaken. Where local rulers could be bribed or otherwise persuaded to collaborate, the role of force was correspondingly diminished.

In general, the resort to force was more marked in colonies of settlement where major efforts had been made to supplant existing modes and patterns of agricultural production and residence. When force was employed, it frequently involved the use of troops recruited locally. If the price were right, some chiefs were as ready to supply troops as they had once been to supply slaves. By 1900, it was possible in some situations, for example, the last campaign against the Asante, to dispense with British troops altogether (Davidson, 1978, p. 85).

If physical rejection of imperial expansion produced a violent and irresistible European response, it is no wonder that many African rulers quickly appreciated that 'the rewards for collaboration were better than the consequences of resistance' (Hodder-Williams, 1984, p.23). It was less a question of collaboration being the lesser of two evils, but rather that the support of the imperial power was seen as an increasingly valuable political and economic resource. Through collaboration, chiefs and other rulers often succeeded in retaining their traditional authority while enjoying preferential access to new sources of wealth and power. The scale and range of opportunities clearly varied, but among the new rewards can be included direct payments for services, access to tax revenues, salaries and the transformation of customary economic rights.

It was common for chiefs to receive rebates for tax collection and, in the French colonies, such rebates continued until after the Second World War. Direct payments to chiefs in Sierra Leone began in 1896 and continued until the 1930s. Such payments were further supplemented by annual gifts and entertainment allowances (Cartey and Kilson (eds), 1966). As chiefs consolidated themselves within the new colonial administrative framework, they were able to generate additional income by illicit manipulation of the taxing power and by converting customary rights to tribute and labour into cash payments. Such developments ensured that traditional rulers were strategically placed at an early stage to exploit the opportunities presented by the colonial economy.

The feasibility of working through traditional authorities, what later became known as Indirect Rule, clearly depended on the availability and pliability of suitable local elites. Where such elites were available, reciprocal benefits could be derived from helping to protect and strengthen their positions. The likely success of such a strategy was obviously related to the character of particular colonies but, where traditional forms of rule had been markedly hierarchical, it was at least possible to conceal partially the extent of imperial manipulation. Indirect Rule had particular attractions in administering colonies of relatively little economic significance but, for obvious reasons, it was inappropriate for settler colonies.

The decision on how best to govern a colony was, with important exceptions, a pragmatic one. In most cases, a virtue was made of necessity and it was not until the 1920s that Lugard codified the principles of Indirect Rule. The consequence, in Davidson's apt phrase, (1978, p.93) was that 'opportunism emerged as doctrine' and attempts were made to impose the system in areas which lacked appropriate authority structures. In some cases, it was thought desirable to invent 'chiefs' but they, not surprisingly, suffered something of a credibility problem. (6)

When European expansion developed an overtly political as well as commercial character, one major result was the creation of new political boundaries. The imposition of arbitrary boundaries to demarcate European possessions served not only to divide communities, but it established new and enduring frames of reference for political and economic activity. Political and economic issues were to be resolved within externally imposed limits which reflected European rather than African concerns and priorities.

The new colonies acquired a new political order and an administrative apparatus which essentially excluded Africans from effective participation. Despite the important differences between, for example, British and French forms of colonial government, the new political orders shared some important characteristics. Government was paternalistic rather than participatory and it was founded on the superior wisdom of the governors rather than on the consent of the governed. The basically authoritarian pattern of colonial rule ensured that bureaucratic structures would predominate. The basic problem was seen as one of translating imperial preferences into administrative reality, of imposing enlightened policies on backward and sometimes recalcitrant peoples. Over time, such perspectives seem unlikely to condition bureaucrats to hold either political leaders or the general public in high esteem and the inculcation of such attitudes and values was to have an enduring impact on the conduct of government in Africa.

For present purposes, it is important to note both the considerable economic impact of colonial rule and the creation of essentially bureaucratic states. It may be true that 'the vast majority of Africans went into colonialism with a hoe and came out with a hoe' (Rodney, 1972, p 239), but this does not mean that the economic effects of colonial rule were either superficial or transitory. All colonial governments were exploitive in the sense that they extracted, or attempted to extract, sufficient revenue from the peasantry to pay at least for the costs of administration. This goal was achieved through a number of mechanisms including forced labour, taxation, land expropriation and military conscription. A combination of these and other measures served to drive many Africans into the cash and wage economy of the colonial power.

The economies of colonies were aligned so far as possible either to meet the commercial needs of the 'mother' country or to generate revenue. In some cases, this required the creation of a pool of wage labourers to work in European owned mines or on European owned plantations. In other cases, the imposition of hut and poll taxes forced peasants to abandon subsistence agriculture in favour of the production of designated cash crops. As we have seen, those African elites who collaborated with colonial governments were well placed to take advantage of the new opportunities and this partly accounts for the differing reactions to colonial rule. Thus, as some groups grew richer, other groups lacked either capital or access to economic and educational opportunities.

The economic impact of colonial rule is scarcely to be explained primarily as the provision of unparalleled economic opportunities for Africans. (7) In practice, not only were such opportunities confined to an elite, but there were strict limits imposed on the range of economic endeavour open even to the most privileged Africans. Even where Africans responded to the new incentives, they were not often allowed to enjoy the full fruits of their efforts. Peasant farmers in Uganda greatly increased their production of cotton, but they were not allowed to participate in cotton-ginning which remained an Asian and European monopoly. The effect of such racially inspired interventions was to stunt and distort the growth of an African capitalist class. Denied access to refining and processing activities, entrepreneurial Africans turned to transport and trading and acted as intermediaries between African cash-crop producers and the foreign controlled import-export companies.

It should perhaps be noted that the notion of 'opportunity' can be both a euphemism and a rationalisation. Where Africans were driven from their land to work in the wage economy for the privilege of paying taxes to meet the expenses of colonial administration, it seems unlikely that they always appreciated fully the 'opportunities' they had been given. The recruiter and the conscript rarely see the induction process in the same light.

The economic change wrought by colonial rule served to stratify further African societies. This accentuated the gulf between local elites and the peasantry but, of more immediate importance, it broadened the horizons of the elites and 'sub-elites' and raised their expectations of government. Having shared in the sometimes substantial crumbs from the European table, they began to press for what they increasingly saw as their rightful share. Thus, they pressed, not to overthrow the colonial system, but to reform it by allowing selected Africans greater economic, educational and administrative opportunities. They sometimes seemed more offended by the increasing discrimination in employment against educated Africans than they were by the lack of educational opportunities available to the general population.

The groups which had adapted to the new opportunities were more likely to attack vigorously the racial barriers to African advance and, in so doing, they sometimes found themselves in the delicate position of acting as spokesmen for much larger groupings whose aspirations were of a rather different order. The result was that some of the early nationalist movements were, or appeared to be, 'elitist in form and conservative in ideology' (Hodder-Williams, 1984, p.72). Where ruling groups had resisted modernising influences, they tended,as in Northern Nigeria, to try to preserve the status quo rather than accelerate the pace of political struggle. Fearful of losing their pre-eminence and political control, they opposed the nationalist agitation of the more developed regions of Nigeria.

Those elements who had done relatively well under colonial rule were naturally anxious to ensure that they continued to enjoy their prosperity and privileges in the future. Their obvious choice of strategy was to make sure that the appropriate structures of the colonial state were preserved intact rather than consumed in the fires of nationalist zeal. Thus, nationalist movements required organisation, guidance and discipline. They needed to be targeted at particular grievances and, because destruction precludes inheritance, they were discouraged from undermining the foundations of the state.

In many African colonies, there was competition for political leadership and rival nationalist parties emerged. Some were so overtly elitist and conservative that, as in the Gold Coast, they were outflanked by more radical organisations. (8). But, in many cases, a combination of legal restrictions, low levels of literacy, poor communications and limited mobility ensured that party differences were based more on ethnic, regional and personal considerations than on ideological differences. The submergence of ideological division in favour of regional and ethnic groupings contributed in some part to converting the struggle for independence into a 'dogfight for the spoils' (Davidson, 1978, p. 237).

The rhetoric of nationalism served to disguise important ideological differences and, in their initial attempts to resist nationalist demands, the imperial powers often imprisoned those they later described as models of moderate and responsible African leadership. Although this leadership was often personally and practically dedicated to the virtues of self-help and private enterprise, their rhetoric was political rather than economic and focused particularly on the need to transfer power into African hands.

In practice, nationalism in a colony the size of Nigeria meant regionalism and competition for spoils. In many of the French colonies, the situation was very different and the colonial power maintained the integrity of a number of small states of dubious viability. In so doing, the French colonies were effectively 'balkanised' and consequently they were always likely to be vulnerable to economic and political pressure and manipulation.

But whatever the sources and forms of political competition in pre-independence Africa, government responsibilities remained in the day to day care of the colonial bureaucracies. The character of such bureaucracies and the forces working within and upon them contributed in large measure to the growth of corruption. To understand how this growth occurred, it is important to grasp both the internal structural features of the bureaucracies and the central role they played in colonial societies. It will be necessary later in this chapter to assess the impact of independence on African bureaucracies and its implications for the growth of corruption.

Regardless of the form of colonial rule, African colonies were governed at the highest levels by Europeans. To attract officials of a suitable calibre in appropriate numbers, it was thought necessary to offer a generous employment package in terms of salaries, accommodation and other benefits. The net result was that Europeans working in Africa probably earned more than their equivalents in Europe. In the later stages of colonial rule, it seemed important to ensure that the remuneration was pitched high enough to induce key European officials to manage the transfer of power. Thus, not only was a high initial standard of remuneration established during the early phases of colonial rule, but it was maintained subsequently and even enhanced as independence approached. (9)

Europeans 'administered' Africa in much the same way as they 'climb' Mount Everest, that is with considerable local help and assistance. It was necessary from the beginning of colonial rule to recruit local agents, interpreters, soldiers, policemen and clerks. These 'sub-elites' grew steadily in size and political and economic importance. As we have seen, chiefs and other rulers were often effectively co-opted as civil servants to extract forced labour, to raise taxes and to maintain order. Nowhere in tropical Africa were Europeans numerous enough to occupy more than the senior levels of bureaucracy. Over time, and particularly after 1945, the demand for African labour grew and diversified.

While the remuneration of European officials in Africa was determined by European standards, the wages of the African employees of the colonial state were established according to the local labour market. To attract clerks and other workers, it was necessary to offer wages which compared very favourably with the rewards available to the cash-crop and subsistence farmer. Thus, the wage rates were set in relation to the alternative employment opportunities for Africans and not to the scales and conditions enjoyed by European officials. While it is not easy to produce convincing statistics to demonstrate these wage relationships, one recent study estimates that the average salary of the African bureaucrat was 5-10 times that of the peasant, but only 20-30% of average European remuneration. (Abernethy, 1983, p.5). Such disparities had important effects on political attitudes and on the demand for educational qualifications.

Investment in African education was only seen as cost-effective by colonial authorities so far as it provided a flow of literate clerks which obviated the need to import larger numbers of relatively expensive European officials. But education was neither completely a government responsibility nor entirely under government control. The charactistic desire to provide African education as cheaply as possible encouraged colonial authorities to transfer much of the burden to Christian missionary organisations. But such bodies possessed goals which stretched beyond supplying the personnel needs of colonial bureaucracies. The result, as Abernethy notes, was that 'government found itself in political difficulty, for the missionaries' interest in proselytization drove them to expand primary and secondary enrollments beyond the level officials considered optimal' (1983, p.6). The supply of educated Africans arriving on the clerical job market began to exceed the demands of both public and private employers. This excess of supply over effective demand had important consequences both for the development of nationalism and for the status of bureaucratic employment.

If the relation between the provision of educational opportunities and the availability of employment opportunities produced frustration and political tensions, the expanding activities of colonial bureaucracies were to have similarly important effects in producing environments conducive to corruption. In particular, the accelerated growth after 1945 of marketing boards and state corporations not only emphasised the pivotal role of governmental and quasi-governmental bodies in economic affairs, but it also provided a widening range of opportunities for corruption to flourish.

Marketing boards, such as the Gold Coast Coca Marketing Board established in 1947, served as a link between the peasant producers of cash-crops and the export market which produced the revenues necessary to pay for the administration of the colony. In providing a guaranteed price and outlet for peasant produce, the marketing boards ostensibly offered a degree of financial stability and certainty, but it is more than possible that such advantages were often obtained at considerable cost to the farmers. The prices paid to peasant farmers tended to be significantly below export prices and the differences constituted a major source of government revenue. Instead of taxing peasants directly and possibly incurring their wrath, both colonial governments and their African successors found it highly convenient to extract revenues indirectly through the pricing policies of the marketing boards. Such revenues could be devoted to a range of sometimes dubious purposes including supporting a burgeoning bureaucracy in the manner to which it was becoming accustomed or swelling the campaign treasury of the dominant political party.

If colonial governments and the emergent African leadership had different uses for the funds generated by the marketing boards, neither was in a position to combat effectively the growing corruption associated with the boards' activities. Board officials inevitably had dealings 'not only with individual farmers and petty entrepreneurs, but with a wide variety of local farmers' associations, as well as with cartels of market-women, transporters, petty traders and wholesalers' (LeVine, 1975, p.18). The point here is that the aim of the marketing boards was to disturb and disrupt established trading relationships and those groups which profited from such relationships were often ready and able to use illicit means to sustain them. It seems clear that, even before independence, there was considerable corruption in the workings of the marketing boards.

As the colonial period drew to a close, the picture which emerged in, for example, the Gold Coast, had two major aspects. At the lower levels, officials were involved in corrupt private deals with farmers and businessmen anxious to avoid the regulations and financial burdens imposed by the marketing boards, while, at the higher levels, the officials of the Convention Peoples' Party were siphoning off considerable revenues to bolster campaign funds and distribute as patronage. As independence approached, access to marketing board funds became almost the sine qua non of political organisation and success.

B. Implications and consequences

In one sense, colonialism pervaded all aspects of African life. It transformed trade, agriculture, transport, government, education and patterns of settlement. Yet what is particularly striking and important about the colonial experience is how uneven and partial were its effects. Most directly, colonialism established a new alien ruling class which was imposed on unwilling peoples who recognised neither the legitimacy nor the desirability of the new political order. Africans discovered that their lives were regulated in a variety of new ways and restrictions were placed on their right to live and work where and how they pleased.

The new rulers were, of course, almost impotent without the co-operation of African elites and sub-elites. For a minority of Africans, colonial rule offered unprecedented opportunities for education, employment and entrepreneurial endeavour. One consequence was an increased stratification of African societies and the growing contrast between the new bureaucratic classes and the ordinary peasants became ever more clearer. It soon became evident that 'Even in the most backward areas of the bush everyone has grasped the fact that the official with clean hands earns more and works much less' (Dumont, 1966, p. 88).

The implications of the contrast between peasants and

bureaucrats were clear. While the peasant was poor and powerless, the bureaucrat was affluent and authoritative. Given such disparities, peasants sought access to bureaucrats and the resources they commanded. Almost inevitably, bribery was the obvious means of gaining short-term access and of establishing a sympathetic relationship with bureaucrats. Officials were to be placated and not confronted. Confrontation with bureaucracy was fraught with risks and dangers and therefore to be avoided because, as the Ashanti proverb warns, 'A man does not rub bottoms with a porcupine'.

While bribery offered to many, if not to the very poor, a means of temporary and limited access to government favour and resources, a more permanent and substantial type of access was not merely to influence bureaucrats, but to become one. If this route was closed even to richer peasants because of their lack of educational qualifications, it could be opened for their offspring. It thus became imperative to ensure that children had access to appropriate educational opportunities. In practice, the striking attractions of a bureaucratic career were so great that they excited an apparently insatiable demand for the kinds of education which provided access to government employment. The immediate pressure for expanding and inexpensive primary school systems was soon matched by a growing emphasis on the need for opportunities in higher education. The rewards for a graduate civil servant were so great that they served as a powerful incentive. In 1962, the initial salary of an Honours graduate in Kenya was nine times that of an Ungraded Clerk (Abernethy, 1983 p.9).

The gross disparities in the rewards available to peasants and bureaucrats, together with the wide differentials operating within colonial bureaucracies, virtually ensured that both access to education and recruitment and advancement within the civil service would be subject to corrupt influence. After independence, the income differentials were more often confirmed than condemned. The new governments gave a high priority to Africanising senior posts and expanding their bureaucracies and they made little effort to redress a situation in which top officials sometimes earned over one hundred times more than the average peasant.

Thus far, the analysis has focused principally on the important links between the objectives of colonial rule, the restructuring of colonial economies to meet these objectives, and the form and character of the bureaucracies created to ensure the implementation of colonial policies. We have seen that one consequence was to multiply the opportunities for corruption through the activities of marketing boards and other regulatory bodies. We have also seen that the kinds of bureaucracies which developed in most African states provided classic breeding grounds for what might be called the politics of envy. The stark contrasts between the lives of peasants and the urban unemployed and the lifestyles of both junior and senior bureaucrats provided compelling incentives for corruption. In assessing the impact of colonialism on the growth of corruption, it therefore seems clear that it profoundly altered the structure and scale of incentives, opportunities and rewards.

If economic factors have played an important role in encouraging and facilitating the growth and spread of corruption, the differing attitudes and aspirations of nationalist politicians and party officials have made their own contributions to the process. The process of decolonisation obviously varied considerably and so too did subsequent relationships with the former colonial powers. Where independence was only won after armed struggle, as in the Portugese colonies, it encouraged the political mobilisation of the peasantry and the emergence of a markedly more radical African leadership. Conversely, by securing relatively rapid and peaceful decolonisation, colonial powers were able to retain privileged relationships with many of the new African governments. In some cases, as in Kenya, it was possible for the colonial power to survive a period of violent rebellion and still manage to transfer power to suitably co-operative nationalist politicians.

The ambitions of nationalist politicians sometimes seemed to be confined to the substitution of black faces for white ones in positions of political authority. But where the goal was to dismantle the structure of the colonial state and to re-distribute resources and opportunities, decolonisation proved to be a bitter and protracted process. In either case, there were important implications for the social, economic and political character of the new states.

In practice, armed struggle was the exception and, on occasion, the nationalist movements were anti-colonial in only the most formal of senses. In cases where the mass of the population remained politically unmobilised, nationalist politicians formed alliances with traditional rulers, for example, the inaccurately named Sierra Leone Peoples' Party had links with the paramount chiefs but almost no significant rural organisation. The point here is that it was not uncommon for the nationalist leadership to be unrepresentative of, and unresponsive to, grassroots opinion. Differences in origin, status and objective were later to have important consequences for the conduct of government and for public responses to it.

Unsurprisingly, nationalist activists were often those who stood to gain most out of independence. When upward mobility was blocked by racial discrimination, inadequate educational provision and the limited field of activity of colonial bureaucracies, nationalist leaders found it easy to recruit their anti-colonial vanguard. It became ever more clearer that the fruits of office were likely to prove considerable and, as independence approached, 'the more intense became the competition between individuals, factions and (most dangerously) ethnic, regional and religious groups over who was going to enjoy them (Clapham, 1985, p.32). Where the political succession was clear at an early stage, the dominant party, for example, the Convention Peoples Party in the Gold Coast, moved quickly to acquire the financial resources of the government to reinforce their position.

To generate popular support, nationalist leaders were obliged to assert that independence would substantially improve the material lot of the indigenous populations. Once the transfer of power was complete, the new governments naturally came under pressure to deliver on their promises. The most immediate and direct sources of pressure were the party officials and activists anxious to taste the fruits of public office as recompense for their contributions in securing independence. A much broader constituency pressed for the promised improvements in, for example, educational provision, health care and better transport facilities. In the short term, it seemed possible for governments to respond to both sources of pressure. If the new governments were expected to extend and develop a wide range of functions on an unprecedented scale, a considerable expansion in the size of the bureaucracy was both justified and inevitable.

In effect, what occurred was a bureaucratic explosion. The parastatals proliferated and central bureaucracies expanded enormously. In almost every case, substantial increases in the numbers employed in the public sector were the order of the day. The already substantial Nigerian bureaucracy increased by 50% in the first five years of independence and, in Senegal, government employment grew from 10,000 before independence to 35,000 in 1965, and to 61,000 in 1973.

Senior African bureaucrats inherited the status and rewards of their European predecessors and their subordinates pressed to close the gap in remuneration between the different levels of the administration hierarchy. The success of such claims resulted not only in a narrowing of differentials, but an increase in administrative costs. More importantly, the differentials between bureaucratic and other forms of employment widened still further. Careers in the burgeoning bureaucracy seemed more attractive than ever and, in the confusion of government expansion, access could readily be effected through illicit inducements. The pressures for bureaucratic employment were so great that the parastatals in particular became, and have remained, grossly overstaffed. The overall impact of these pressures was considerable and produced a situation where 'The salary structure of African governments has helped to transform these governments into powerful interest groups whose overriding interest is themselves' (Abernethy, 1983, p. 15).

While civil servants and parastatal employees were naturally keen to press their claims on the political leadership, they were by no means immune from pressure themselves. Where Africans succeeded in gaining public sector employment, they often came under great pressure from relatives, neighbours, friends and acquaintances to provide favours, jobs and other benefits. In such cases, each official had to find his own way between the formal, legal duties of his public office and the informal, irregular approaches of a small army of social contacts claiming preferential treatment. Inevitably, African officials became entangled in a vortex of conflicting loyalties and pressures.

The imposition of colonial rule disrupted, but did not often completely destroy, established practices and attitudes. European rules and values modified and overlaid African customs, rather than eradicated them. A new value system was imposed which both paralleled and dominated existing systems. One important consequence was that established practices were re-assessed from new perspectives and what had been customary sometimes became illegal. It therefore became possible to transform pre-colonial practices such as customary gift giving into bribery. The partial continuity with the old custom often helped disguise the real nature of the new act. But it is precisely because the colonial impact was neither uniform nor comprehensive that confusion and uncertainty arose about the relation of bureaucratic norms to pre-existing obligations. Thus, instead of one value system directly and completely replacing another, the systems existed partly in isolation from each other and partly in competition. If the competition was unequal, it was nevertheless real.

The African official often found himself in a delicate position. To the extent that he was a member of a wide social network which conferred reciprocal rights and responsibilities, he was not likely to internalise fully the impersonal ethos of Weberian notions of bureaucratic conduct. At one level, officials often owed their status and incomes to their educational qualifications but, more pertinently, they frequently owed their education to the support of their extended family and local community. Obviously, the beneficiary of communal help is placed under a powerful obligation and, in subsequently refusing assistance, he would be violating basic social expectations. It is therefore no surprise that, in Africa, European notions of public office holding are only unevenly and partially ingrained. To many African officials, it seems both natural and proper to use the resources of public office to help relatives and friends in need. Similarly, those who unsuccessfully seek preferential treatment from a bureaucrat are unlikely to commend his integrity. In some circumstances, the refusal of a modest bribe could be construed as a negotiating ploy and as indicative of greed rather than of honesty and incorruptability.

If social pressures were frequently powerful enough to override any Weberian notions of bureaucratic loyalty and responsibility, there were other important factors which encouraged both politicians and officials to denigrate public duty and service in favour of personal enrichment. The new states were, after all, European creations based on arbitrary and artificial boundaries. Thus, it could not be assumed that the inhabitants would be united by any sense of mutual interest, shared history or common destiny. In practice, status and influence were locally acquired and enjoyed and, as a consequence, the locality rather than the nation was the normal focus of loyalty and support. The absence of any widely shared concepts of citizenship, brotherhood or national interest implied that people of different ethnic groups, religions, regions or localities were more vulnerable to exploitation. To most Africans, the nation was a vague and meaningless abstraction and government was a remote and alien tyranny whose resources were a legitimate target for diversion and re-distribution.

While the colonial state has been substantially expanded and modified to meet the demands of independence, it is not immediately obvious that perceptions of the proper relationship between ruler and ruled have been similarly altered. The new African leadership has tended to exhibit a similar sense of superiority over those whom they rule. Government is seen as the province of the governors rather than the governed and it is therefore perceived more as a question of facilitating direction from above than of encouraging participation from below.

Where no ties of kin or community bind politicians and their publics, the gulf in status between them tends to strengthen patron-client relations to the consequent detriment of attempts to instill concepts of public service. Similarly, the gulf between ruler and ruled in Africa encourages the ruled to regard government as alien, oppressive and immune from popular control. When governments and their policies are imposed on unwilling peoples, corruption offers one way of mitigating the consequences. Rural people in remote areas may opt to withdraw from the reach of government, but such opportunities to 'exit' are scarcely available to urban dwellers or those otherwise integrated into the economy. If there are no exits, such groups may publicly protest and, where possible, find corrupt methods of making government more responsive and congenial.

In many cases, African leaders inherited colonial structures, practices and attitudes and, although their goals are ostensibly different, it is not always easy to find much evidence of radical change. The economies of most African countries are still structured along the lines established under colonial rule and attempts at industrialisation and diversification have not been conspicuously successful. Peasant producers of cash crops are still receiving substantially less than international market prices for their output because African governments have quickly appreciated the value of a range of regulatory mechanisms for extracting large revenues.

Thus, marketing boards and other parastatals have been established to facilitate control of the import-export trade and to pay for the escalating costs of the administrative apparatus. The surplus extracted from the peasantry is, of course, used to finance a variety of government services and projects, but often much appears to be siphoned off by the ruling group. Where this happens, the contrast with colonial rule is less than clear. While the surpluses once found their way into sterling balances held in London, the post-independence surpluses are partly to be found in personal balances held in Switzerland or Lichtenstein.

In concluding this chapter, it may be useful to draw together some of the threads of the analysis. If corruption involves, in part, bribery and buying the co-operation of those in authority, it was employed from the earliest days of colonial expansion to secure the collaboration of traditional rulers. Western governments and companies have continued to finance those African leaders and organisations which seemed best likely to secure and enhance Western commercial and political interests. Thus, the 'scholarships' made available to aspiring nationalist politicians in the 1950s by American funded trade union organisations are seen by some observers as more or less polite forms of corruption (Davidson, 1978, pp 217-218). The thread which connects the 'scholarship' man to the co-opted chief is not solely Western finance, but the role expected of the beneficiary. In their different ways, it was anticipated that they would act as surrogates for Western control and influence.

It is precisely in this role of intermediary that both African politicians and businessmen have found their most clearly articulated identities. (10) Traditional rulers linked the colonial power to African peoples and enabled it to accomplish economic changes which would otherwise have proved formidable. African businessmen were largely excluded from manufacturing and processing and thus found their most profitable role as traders, distributors and middlemen linking peasant production with European or Levantine export companies and linking importers with the growing urban elite. The post-colonial state has grown apace and the activities of burgeoning bureaucracies intrude at many points in the lives of ordinary people. Oppressive and intrusive bureaucracies in turn engender a need for intermediaries and brokers who can ease or deflect the pressures of government. It seems evident that the overriding demand in African politics, business and administration is for go-betweens, fixers and agents with the relevant and necessary connections to intercede on behalf of those seeking government favour, exemption or support.

From colonial times to the present, the centrality of the state has guaranteed that political and economic life are inescapably intertwined. The pre-eminence and predominance of the state all but precludes the evolution of pluralist political systems and the absence or weakness of competitive organisations and groupings suggests that a potentially important check and restraint on corruption in Africa is missing. As we have noted, African leaders more often inherited than transformed the colonial state and, since independence, they have consolidated and expanded it. The business of Africa is bureaucracy and its scale and extent impedes and inhibits internal challenge or competition. Within such a framework, politicians, civil servants and parastatal employees strive to defend and advance their interests and, in so doing, they necessarily maintain and strengthen their hold on resource extraction and allocation. But if, as seems evident, the economies of many African states can no longer bear the financial burden of their swollen bureaucracies, major changes in resource allocation will have to be made. The prospects for such a re-allocation must be poor when the formal authority to make radical change rests solely with those who have the most to lose.

Government and bureaucracy in Africa have grown, in part, to tackle the problems of independence and development, but the size and appetite of the bureaucratic state has become, in some cases, a major problem in itself. The creation and expansion of the bureaucratic state in Africa has engendered and exacerbated gross inequalities and disparities and a major consequence has been to provide a plethora of incentives and opportunities for corruption.

NOTES

(1)   The stereotype, like the cliche, often contains more than a grain of truth, but it indicates a reluctance to respond to growing complexity and diversity. Among the

stereotypes of relevance here are the ideas that 'traditional' African societies all possessed a collective ethos and lacked both money economies and any awareness of distinctions between public and private purposes.

(2)   The critical reaction has been considerable, but (Frank, 1971; and Smith, 1973) make most of the telling objections.

(3)   This is to say that all definitions of corruption utilise a desired standard of public conduct and thereby limit discretion to pursue personal advantage through the use of public resources.

(4)   The literature on colonial history is, of course vast, but (Fieldhouse, 1982; and Rodney, 1972) make interesting and contrasting starting points.

(5)   Strictly speaking, the terms imperialism and colonialism mean different things in that the former does not require the latter, but the latter requires the former. My use of the terms is fairly loose, but the differing experiences of settler and non-settler territories are examined later.

(6)   The role of such chiefs is discussed by (Tignor in Ekpo (ed), 1979, pp. 189-210). Tignor argues that they were provided with little in the way of supportive or coercive apparatus to carry out their assigned functions. He suggests that 'without corruption, the whole system would have collapsed' (p. 198).

(7)   Excellent analyses of the contrasting experiences in West and East Africa are contained in (Hopkins, 1973; and Brett, 1973).

(8)   Kwame Nkrumah had been secretary to the 'moderate' middle-class United Gold Coast Convention before breaking away to found the more populist and politically effective Convention Peoples' Party. The circumstances surrounding this development are explained in (Apter, 1963; and Austin, 1964).

(9)   For a useful elaboration of these and related issues, see (Bennell, 1982).

(10)   In his classic indictment, Fanon argues, 'The national middle class discovers its historic mission: that of intermediary. Seen though its eyes, its mission has

nothing to do with transforming the nation; it consists
prosaically, of being the transmission link between the
nation and a capitalism, rampant through camouflaged,
which today puts on the masque of neocolonialism'
(Fanon, 1967, p. 122).

4 Modes and mechanisms

Some years ago, a British technician went to a government office in Lusaka to obtain an application form for a driving test. When he presented the completed form to the counter clerk, he was asked to pay a fee of fifty kwache. The fee mentioned on the form was only five kwache but, assuming the form was out of date, the technician duly paid up.

'How long do I have to wait for the driving test?', he inquired. The clerk smiled, 'That was the test. Congratulations, you passed.'

Political corruption is not always as simple, direct and blatant as the above story suggests. It is far from monolithic and, in practice, it takes many forms and occurs in different parts of most African political systems. If the preceding chapter charted the birth and development of corruption, the present chapter explores problems of anatomy and physiology. It examines the key institutional characteristics and other variables which shape the form and location of corruption. For immediate purposes, the analysis is pitched at a general level, but the following chapter illustrates how differing forms and concentrations of corruption evolve in particular political and economic circumstances.

Writers on corruption are much taken with metaphor and analogy. None is more popular than the iceberg which is regularly deployed in service of the conviction that observable corruption is but a small, unrepresentative fragment of the whole. A Ghanaian investigation of corruption reported in 1975, for example, 'We were conscious throughout our inquiry that we were perceiving a kind of iceberg. We could only describe and measure accurately the part above the sea. The great bulk submerged below the sea, we were aware of but could not accurately describe or measure' (Justice P.D. Anin, quoted in West Africa, 18th June, 1979, p. 1063). Given the generally clandestine character and reputation of corruption, it might be supposed that the iceberg is a useful image to disguise a sea of ignorance. It seems reasonable to assume that those found guilty of corruption, like criminals generally, are probably the unlucky, the incompetent and the over-confident. Worrying about the depth of the iceberg is, like fighting over deckchairs on the Titanic, to display a curious sense of priorities. If we accept that the, on occasion, spurious precision of statistical analysis is beyond the reach of the student of corruption, then what we assert about corruption is necessarily of a different order. To speak of the incidence of corruption in particular areas as high or low, as increasing, static or declining is probably to stretch the analytical capabilities of political science to their limits.

Every student of anatomy learns early in their training where to find the vital organs, but to locate the main centres of corruption in a political system is not always as straightforward. Where corruption is discreet, private and confined to a narrow group, it is possible for observers to underestimate, or even overlook, its political and economic importance. Conversely, where it is conspicuous and widely known, its significance may, in certain circumstances, be exaggerated or misunderstood. But many kinds of corruption in Africa are far from clandestine and, together with the sheer scale of illicit activities, this makes it relatively easy to locate and describe its principal forms and arenas.

In Africa and elsewhere, it is the nature and distribution of political power which serves to focus and structure corruption. Like interest group activity, corruption is often a remarkably good indicator of where political and administrative decisions are actually, as opposed to formally, made. Those seeking to influence or corrupt the political process are necessarily attracted to, and are dependent upon, politicians, officials, and judges with the power to make binding discretionary decisions. After all, a bribe mis-directed is a bribe wasted. There is little or no point in bribing someone who, because of party discipline, strict and rigid rules or an interfering superior, is unable to deliver the required service or favour. This is not to deny, of course, that the above excuses are sometimes offered in attempts to solicit increased or extra bribes. Where resources are allocated, burdens imposed and benefits distributed, corruption will not be far behind.

In a corrupt polity, the absence or triviality of corruption in particular institutions or processes can usually be regarded less as a sign of exemplary and unusual integrity than as a positive indication of political impotence. Abstinence or celibacy are perhaps less commendable when there is little or no prospect of temptation. Thus, to observe that legislative corruption is less notorious than other forms in Africa is to say more about the role of legislatures than it is to say anything about corruption. Where legislatures exercise considerable control over the process and content of law-making and where individual legislators can galvanise bureaucracy and redress constituency grievances, one would expect, as in the United States, to find a relatively high incidence of legislative corruption. But the role of legislatures in Africa has generally diminished and they have largely succumbed to the increasing power of executive government. In such circumstances, parliamentary representatives are reduced to fulfilling largely symbolic and supportive functions. Where legislators are still seen as potentially valuable allies, as perhaps in Kenya (1), the incidence of legislative corruption correspondingly increases. In short, as the power and influence of individuals and institutions waxes and wanes, so does the likelihood that corruption will rise and fall.

As political processes and climates change, certain arenas for corrupt activity become unavailable or take on different forms. In the period of intense political competition before independence, electoral malpractice and corruption were outstanding features of political life in Nigeria and in many other African countries. The incidence of such forms of corruption has probably declined in recent years for the excellent reason that competitive elections have become increasingly rare events. If competitive elections occur in situations where the outcome is uncertain, as in Nigeria in 1983, the costs can be considerable. In the Nigerian case, 'The political parties spent lavishly on their elaborate campaigns, money which almost certainly had been siphoned from public treasuries either at the federal or state levels' (West Africa, 1984, p.257). The veteran Nigerian politician, Chief Awolowo, has asserted that 'the election was rigged on a big scale in 1979 and massively rigged in 1983' (quoted in West Africa, 21st November, 1983). When campaign funds are in over-plentiful supply, it appears that they are often diverted to illicit purposes. (2) But even where election results are a forgone conclusion, coercion and bribery are often used to maximise the scale of victory. Sweeping electoral victory, or at least the appearance of it, can be an effective propaganda weapon to bolster the internal and external prestige of the regime. In such contexts, the function of elections is to provide ritual regime support rather that to offer opportunities to make meaningful changes in either political leaderships or public policies.

It seems clear that the parts of political structure which lack power, autonomy and discretion are likely to be relatively free of corruption because buyers are only interested in those who have something to sell. If the American Congress is 'the best legislature money can buy', few African legislatures merit similar investment. The importance of different forms of corruption obviously varies from country to country and it is therefore a mistake to imagine that corruption is uniformly or consistently present in the political systems of Africa. The scope and location of corruption depend on and reflect both the content of public policies and the distribution of decision-making power in each society.

But to recognise that the pattern of corruption varies from country to country is not to deny that there are broad similarities and structural considerations which permit a number of general observations. Most importantly, corruption in Africa appears to be centred principally on the extensive discretionary functions of the executive branch of government. For present purposes, the executive branch may be taken to include the political leadership, whether civilian or military, and the bureaucracy, whether central or local. Political power in Africa is primarily governmental power and this predominance partly confirms the validity of Lord Acton's dictum, 'All power corrupts but absolute power corrupts absolutely'. Given the pre-eminence of the state in African politics and society, it is hardly surprising that there seem to be few alternative means of achieving individual or group goals and little prospect of calling government to account for its conduct of public affairs.

While the leaders of military coups often cite widespread corruption as a justification for their intervention in the political process, there seems to be little evidence to suggest that military governments enjoy any more resistance to corruption than their civilian predecessors. In practice, some of Africa's most corrupt leaders, for example, Mobutu in Zaire and Acheampong in Ghana, have been military men. In the latter case, a regime which purported to purify politics produced such colossal corruption that Ghana slid into 'utter bankruptcy, hyperinflation and an utterly desparate socioeconomic crisis' (Young, 1982, p. 164). It appears that, in most cases, the African military are concerned first and foremost to satisfy their corporate needs and this is reflected in high military spending and other measures intended to raise the status of the army and its leaders. In the last resort, military regimes tend to resist reforms which either encourage political participation or impose restraints on the autonomy of the army.

Having removed the civilian political element by coup d'etat, the military regime often proves to be merely a variant of bureaucratic government and, as such, is susceptible to the weaknesses which have afflicted civilian governments in Africa.

A. Bureaucracy, Organisation and Corruption

Both civilian and military governments require extensive administrative apparatuses and the structural characteristics of these bureaucratic organisations help determine the shape and location of corruption. Most obviously, if corruption flourishes at the point of discretionary decision, then a highly decentralised form of administration is likely to multiply the number of potentially corrupt encounters between officials and citizens. Conversely, where decision-making authority is highly centralised, field officers will be by-passed and favours sought from the more powerful officials in the capital or at regional headquarters. In crude terms, centralisation of bureaucracy helps concentrate corruption while decentralisation disperses it around the country. If corruption is prevalent and entrenched under either form, it becomes very difficult to reform governmental structures and alter the distribution of authority.

If the relationship between centre and periphery influences the location of corruption, the relationships between officials and between different levels of bureaucracy are also of considerable importance. It is particularly relevant to note the differing impacts on corruption of competitive and non-competitive bureaucracies. In competitive bureaucracies, officials responsible for allocating licences or dispensing subsidies enjoy overlapping jurisdictions. When an official demands a bribe from an applicant, the response of the applicant and the size of the bribe is closely related to the prospects of receiving free or cheaper treatment from another official. In such situations, 'a reverse Gresham's Law applies - where the honesty of some officials breeds legality in others' (Rose-Ackerman, 1978, p.138). Competition among applicants creates incentives to offer bribes, but competition among bureaucrats may lead to a decline in bribery or in the level of bribes.

Conversely, in the non-competitive bureaucracy, officials are given a monopoly over a particular clientele. The consequence is that those who rely on specific bureaucratic services are completely dependent on the probity of the official assigned to their case or application. Weber's classic account of bureaucracy asserts that a careful division of bureaucratic responsibility is more efficient and avoids wasteful duplication (3) but, in Africa, it has the effect of strengthening the position of the corrupt official. The lesson seems to be that order, neatness and precision in the organisation of bureaucracy and the allocation of authority may facilitate rather than frustrate corrupt transactions. In essence, the exercise of bureaucratic discretion is a manifestation of monopoly power and this encourages and simplifies the organisation of corruption.

African bureaucracies are ostensibly hierarchical. The decisions of low-level officials are formally subject to review by higher-level officials. This power can be used by civil servants to root out corruption, but it is equally available for co-opting or buying off subordinates. Where decisions are regularly reviewed by senior officials, the utility of bribery is related more to the honesty or otherwise of the senior than the junior official. Conversely, if there are no or few rights of appeal to higher authorities, the junior official's bargaining position is correspondingly enhanced. It seems to follow that where senior officials are known to be corrupt, junior ones are unlikely to remain honest. Similarly, where low-level corruption is widespread, senior officials are also likely to be corrupt. The chain of command which links the administrative hierarchy serves to ensure that no level of bureaucracy is invulnerable to corruption. Reducing opportunities for corruption at one level of the hierarchy may reduce corruption, but more often it transfers its focus to a different level.

The relationship of different levels of bureaucracy depends in part on mutual expectations. If superiors are considered corrupt and the refusal of a bribe simply re-directs it to higher levels, the honest junior official becomes a rare animal. Where superiors are relatively honest, but suspect their juniors of corruption or incompetence, they are unlikely to be willing to delegate authority. The failure to delegate produces the familiar spectacle in African government offices of small armies of applicants and supplicants waiting to see the boss, 'the big man', the official who can actually make things happen. But the greater the burden of work and the volume of demands placed on senior officials, the more likely they are to employ competitive bribery as a decision-making device. In cases where technical expertise is in short supply and senior officials do not possess the knowledge or information to evaluate competing tenders for development projects, the resort to competitive bribery as a means of awarding contracts may be more pronounced. Despite the unwillingness to delegate authority, no senior official or head of department is entirely master of his own timetable or agenda. All bureaucracies require 'gatekeepers' who structure access to senior officials. This function may become the responsibility of junior officials, but in Africa it is often assumed by outside brokers, lobbyists and intermediaries who thrive on their ability to secure privileged access to decision-makers. Those requiring access are compelled to pay tolls to pass the relevant political and administrative 'gates'.

The analysis thus far has focused on questions of organisational structure, but the above generalisations are especially applicable to bureaucracies which exhibit more or less regular and predictable patterns of behaviour. The problem in analysing African bureaucracies is that they sometimes display only a limited, or even passing, resemblance to Weber's ideal type. The qualities of precision, control, responsibility, regularity and certainty allegedly possessed by the ideal type of bureaucracy are often conspicuous by their absence in the African context. In practice, precision and control are unobtainable because African bureaucracies operate in conditions of chaos and confusion. In some cases, a large proportion of the bureaucracy exist only as names on pay packets or salary cheques. In 1979, President Mobutu alleged that 'budget cuts of two thirds could be made very easily in Zaire simply by eliminating fictitious employees' (Gould, 1980, p.71). In this extreme case, where at least half the civil service exists only in the imagination of their colleagues, it seems improbable that the alleged advantages of large-scale bureaucracy will be fully realised. (4)

This is not to assert that all African bureaucracies are as disorganised and chaotic as the Zairean, but rather to note that the advantages which flow from the ideal type are subject to specific conditions of a kind not commonly found in Africa. Abrupt and frequent changes of regime, shifting and blurring lines of authority and the fusion of the political and administrative combine to ensure that, in Africa, bureaucracies are likely to remain immature, underdeveloped and unstable.

Given the prevailing level of disorganisation, certain responses and attitudes to corruption have become generally ingrained. When government administration is lax and uncertain, files are frequently mislaid or 'lost', perhaps even sent to imaginary civil servants. Rather than take a chance on the 'system' processing an application for a licence or subsidy, the prudent applicant is willing to pay for a more 'personal' and reliable service. When those responsible for a civil service are not even aware, within generous tolerances, of the number and identity of their employees, the risks of engaging in corrupt transactions are unlikely to be very high. If internal efficiency is low, administrative boundaries uncertain and public offices invaded by tidal waves of dubious middlemen, it seems unlikely that either citizen or bureaucrat will possess a very clear view of what constitutes acceptable conduct. In the presence of administrative confusion and the absence of recognised standards, behaviour of only slightly or moderately dubious propriety is likely to go unnoticed and unpunished.

It seems clear that, given the scarcity of government resources in Africa in relation to the demands on those resources, attempts will frequently be made to secure corruptly what has been denied openly. It also seems clear that the chronic confusion and inefficiency of administration produces bribery in the form of 'speed' money or dash. But while the circumstances in which most African bureaucracies find themselves certainly engender an increased demand for corrupt transactions, the same circumstances also make it more difficult for corrupt officials, whatever the inducement, to deliver the desired services. Thus, the desire for corrupt services may be matched by a desire to provide such services, but the transactions are not consumated because of scarce resources or chaotic organisation. At the highest levels, bribes are not always paid directly to secure, for example, construction contracts, but to purchase a seat at the negotiating table. Once again, access to decision-makers is a prize in itself and one that is often available at the right price. But access does not guarantee or constitute a bargain because access may be granted to a number of contending parties. In such circumstances, the successful contractor may well have survived two rounds of bribery, one for access and one for the contract itself. Needless to say, allowance for such 'miscellaneous expenses, fees and commissions' is made in the tender price.

The major issue in analysing corruption and bureaucracy in Africa is to identify the direction of the causal influences. Is it the case that corruption has flourished because, in chaotic and disorganised bureaucracies, it offers the possibility of making at least part of the structure work? Alternatively, is the confusion and inefficiency of Africa's bureaucracies a product or consequence, rather than a cause, of corruption? There are no simple answers to such questions and the issue will be further discussed but, for the present, it is worth considering whether the alternative explanations are necessarily mutually exclusive. In short, is corruption both cause and effect rather than cause or effect?

It appears that, in many cases, corruption arises through scarcity of resources rather than inefficiency, incompetence or delay in decision-making and resource allocation. It also seems that, even without corruption, the shortages of skilled manpower and the innumerable demands made on African bureaucracies combine to ensure that administration is unlikely to reach the highest standards of efficiency, effectiveness and dispatch. It was noted in the preceding chapter that corruption grew as the size and responsibility of bureaucracy grew. In consequence, there are no examples in Africa of large-scale bureaucracies performing extensive functions which are, or were, immune or otherwise conspicuously resistant to corruption. If the world were different, it would not be the same and the absence of contrasting models in Africa makes it more difficult to disentangle the explanatory threads. African bureaucracies are both corrupt **and** disorganised and therefore to measure the impact of the one on the other when they are constituent parts of the same situation is highly problematic.

It is possible to argue that, where a bureaucracy is hopelessly disorganised, corruption may help to create some kind of bureaucratic order out of chaos and it is conceivable that this corrupt order provides a possible opportunity to reform and restructure administrative apparatus. By imparting some shape and order to bureaucracy, corruption may paradoxically create the pre-conditions for efforts to reduce corruption. But, in less extreme circumstances, corruption itself may be the primary obstacle to increased administrative efficiency. A provisional assessment must be that attempts to reduce corruption in the hope of improving efficiency and attempts to improve efficiency in the expectation that this will reduce corruption ignore or underestimate the extent to which questions of bureaucracy and corruption are indissoluble.

Corruption in Africa is primarily located in the executive branch of government for the obvious reason that the legislative and judicial branches have generally lost whatever independence and power they may have once possessed. The foregoing analysis has been concerned to explore, in general terms, the structural characteristics of African bureaucracies and to stress the gulf between African practice and the Weberian ideal-type. The next part of this chapter takes a closer look at the dynamics of specific forms of corrupt relationships and the identities of the principal actors involved.

B. Forms and Mechanisms

There seems little doubt that by far the greatest amount of corruption in Africa, if not the most important, takes the form of petty bribery involving those relatively junior government employees who are in regular contact with members of the public. This form of corruption is a feature of everyday life in Africa and, while it may not be endorsed by public opinion, it is sufficiently entrenched as to form part of popular expectations of bureaucratic behaviour. For many Africans, petty bribery has become a natural and ingrained feature of their dealings with bureaucracy.

In some cases, bribery is more accurately described as extortion in that it is less a case of officials succumbing to temptation than a question of demanding payment for services they are legally obliged to provide without charge. In other circumstances,

bribery is more difficult to categorise and it can be likened to
the chicken and egg conundrum in that it is not always possible to
say whether the offer of, or the demand for, the bribe came first.
When a new official is offered his first bribe, he may be
offended, even insulted. He learns that, not only are such bribes
regularly offered, but they are regularly accepted by his
colleagues and his attitude is likely to change to conform to the
expectations and general practice of both colleagues and clients.
Over time, he accepts bribery as a normal and natural method of
doing business and, on the occasion when no offer of a bribe is
forthcoming, he is likely to demand one. Similarly, when
confronting an official whose co-operation is required, it becomes
customary to offer a bribe both to obtain more sympathetic
treatment and because the official expects it. Not offering a
bribe runs the double risk of offending the official and allowing
the official to set an unrealistically high price for his
co-operation.

Not all petty bribery involves bureaucrats, indeed, in some
African countries, police and army corruption is as prominent a
feature of public life. Driving in countries such as Zaire, Nigeria
or Liberia, it is not at all uncommon to encounter unauthorised
roadblocks manned by men in military attire who extract payment
from each passing motorist, taxi driver and bus passenger. (5)
The success of such illegal tollgates is greatly enhanced by the
possession and threatening display of automatic weapons. But it is
not always entirely clear whether those who dress as, and purport
to be, soldiers actually are members of the armed forces. What
looks like bribery is often no more than armed robbery
particularly when, for example, in Nigeria, 'uniforms and weapons
are easily rented for an operation by the poorly-paid rank and file
of the forces' (West Africa, February 26th, 1979, p.330). But, in
the ordinary course of events, the military are not strategically
well placed to extract bribes. They are often quartered away
from large urban centres and their normal range of functions is
generally too narrow to encourage or facilitate the development of
a variety of enduring corrupt relationships.

Conversely, the police are in a unique position both to
encourage the offering of bribes and to extort them. Their
contact with a wide cross-section of the public is more frequent
and extensive than that of the military. The broad range of
police responsibilities and the degree of discretion inevitably
afforded those who work on their own initiative help create a
climate in which police officers susceptible to illicit inducements
are able to succumb with a measure of impunity.

The police officer represents the authority of the law and, in
most encounters, he is an authority on the law. The police
possess not only the intimidating powers of arrest and detention,

but the ability to set in motion the coercive and regulatory activities of other public bodies such as tax inspectors and customs officials. New police officers are introduced to, and initiated in, the corrupt practices which operate in any particular setting and there are powerful pressures on recruits to conform to peer group norms. If complaints are made against a corrupt police officer, he can rely on peer group solidarity to protect him in all but the most extreme circumstances as, for example, when the aggrieved party has powerful political connections. Complainants are well aware that, even if a specific complaint is upheld and the grievance redressed, they will always be prime targets for police reprisals. Given such knowledge, attempted and actual extortions by police, especially in urban centres, may receive press publicity, but it goes largely unreported in official channels.

Some sections of the population are both more likely to offer bribes and have bribes extorted from them. Criminals and those who operate on the threshold of legality or beyond, for example, gamblers, prostitutes, bar and nightclub owners, are peculiarly vulnerable to the depredations of the police. In such circumstances, complaints about police extortion are often tantamount to self-incrimination. The police therefore have a vested interest in opposing the de-criminalisation of those activities where widespread bribery occurs.

Like their military counterparts, the police frequently resort to the use of roadblocks for the purpose of extracting unauthorised tolls. Unlike the army, they tend to rely less on an open display of armed force to extract payments, than on their power to enforce regulations relating to the construction and use of vehicles. Readers familiar with the chronic over-crowding and over-loading of buses and lorries in West Africa will immediately recognise that the police have ample scope. The general problems associated with vehicle maintenance and with the supplies of spares for European and Japanese vehicles in Africa are such that the police do not find it excessively difficult to compile a list of possible vehicle faults. If overcrowding and poor maintenance are unavoidable, so are illicit payments to police (6).

Within the bureaucracy, two classes of official are particularly well placed to attract and extract bribes. The first are customs officials who have the right to refuse entry or exit to persons and goods and who have discretion in the impositions of duties and taxes. At the very least, they can subject travellers to inordinate delays, personal searches and other forms of obstruction and humiliation. Businessmen who wish to circumvent stringent exchange control regulations and traders and farmers anxious to export produce rather than sell it at state controlled prices are all willing to pay customs officials to cultivate a Nelsonian view of their activities. Those engaged in illicit enterprises and tired travellers are particularly vulnerable to the depredations of less than scrupulous customs officials. As we shall see later, the growth and extent of smuggling in Africa has made customs services prime centres of corrupt activity.

The second class of officials strategically placed to supplement their incomes are those concerned with licensing and regulating trading opportunities where the demand actually or artificially exceeds the designated supply. If a woman wishes to join the ranks of the market 'mammies' of Accra, she will need a licence to open her stall. But the number of licences available in this and other markets is generally inadequate to satisfy the number of applications. Some procedure for allocating scarce resources, in this case the market licence, is necessary and competitive bribery often resolves the problem of rationing. The unsuccessful applicants have an alternative course of action and competing demands on their financial resources. The alternative is to open an unlicensed stall, defend it against irate competitors and bribe the 'queen mother', the market inspectors and police to prevent prosecution and expulsion.

The bureaucrat, the soldier and the police officer represent no external constituency and they are answerable, if at all, only to their superiors. Their reputations are not public, but organisational, and the good opinion of their superiors can often be bought. Conversely, the party politician or official is dependent, at least to some degree, on maintaining popular support and approval. While the soldier or police officer may be preoccupied with personal gain, the party politician has to ensure that his more important and influential supporters receive some share of the proceeds of corruption. The party politician retains or enhances his position in the hierarchy by demonstrating to the party leadership that he enjoys the enthusiastic support of his constituents. To maintain a high level of local support, he will be expected both to spend freely and make generous personal donations to local projects as well as obtain preferential access for his constituents to government services and benefits.(7)

The above analysis has been primarily concerned with bribery but, at this point, it may be useful to make some preliminary points about nepotism. While bribery and nepotism are distinct analytical categories, in practice, they are often intimately connected. In describing the growth of corruption, much emphasis was laid on the increasing centrality of the state as a provider of education, employment and economic opportunity. In consequence, it is important to remember that public employees actively engaged in soliciting bribes are likely to be subject to intense pressures to share their good fortune. The ties of blood and community encourage and sometimes demand nepotism. But, as kinship or tribal sentiments weaken in the process of what is sometimes misleadingly called modernisation, the official's sense of communal obligation may be fused with an increasingly clear perception of self-interest. In such cases, the official will continue to give his relatives preference in employment, but he may also demand some kind of fee or proportion of their salary as partial recompense for his generosity.

In certain circumstances, nepotism is a narrow form of patronage. In evaluating applicants for jobs, import licences or agricultural subsidies, competence and technical merit are often not the most important consideration to the employer or official. Where regimes lack stability or any clearly defined and accepted ideological doctrine, there is a continuing difficulty in ensuring that subordinates and superiors work together for common goals. Where organisations such as the army or police have lost or never acquired an esprit de corps, methods have to be found to give individuals a reason to co-operate. Thus, in the above circumstances, nepotism and patronage may serve as substitutes for indoctrination. Political leaders doubtful about the loyalty and support of their lieutenants frequently find that a dash of nepotism makes them feel more secure. (8) Where the ideological cement is too porous to bind leaders and followers together, ties of blood and money must suffice.

Opportunities for bribery and nepotism increase as the scope and size of government expand. During the colonial phase, it was sometimes possible for even large sections of the population to remain relatively unaware of and unaffected by the activities of the colonial government. Such isolation and immunity has largely evaporated and government now impinges more widely and more noticeably and, therefore, the frequency and range of contacts between citizens and officials has increased enormously. If one consequence of the massive expansion in the activities of government is to multiply opportunities for corruption, the absence or weakness of countervailing pressures implies that the incidence of corruption is likely to increase in proportion to the opportunities available. As government expands, the impossibility of framing rules and regulations to meet every circumstance or contingency becomes ever clearer and discretionary decision making power is increasingly devolved to often quite junior officials.

The ingenuity of officials in exploiting their public positions knows few limits. Sometimes it involves officials colluding to appropriate state funds, but often it involves extortion from colleagues, private individuals and companies. Opportunities for corruption arise in the ordinary course of business and in relation to specific and substantive programmes and projects. A recent study (Gould, 1980, pp.123-150) provides a detailed account of the variety of corrupt mechanisms in operation in Zaire. Zaire is probably an extreme case, but some of the transactions and techniques identified by Gould are commonly found elsewhere in Africa. It is by no means unusual, for example, to find that the reason why a senior official never keeps his appointments is because he is away from the office conducting private business on government time. The practice of officials enjoying extensive outside interests is particularly frowned upon in some societies, for example, Tanzania, but there is no doubt that it is widespread in Kenya, Zaire and most of West Africa. There is equally little doubt that such extra-curricula activities are made especially profitable by exploiting official connections and resources.

It is not unknown for senior officials to engage in what is sometimes called 'no-fault blackmail' which simply means that in order for a junior official to remain in the public service, let alone secure advancement, his superiors require some financial reward. In the more extreme cases, junior officials pay senior officials to secure postings where they will enjoy greater access to bribes or opportunities for foreign travel with access to hard currency. Moonlighting and 'no-fault blackmail' are perhaps among the most conspicuous techniques for accumulating capital within Africa's bureaucracies but, as Gould and others have shown, the misuse of public office in Africa takes on an almost infinite variety of forms.

C. Imports and Exports

The discussion thus far in this chapter has had four main themes; to analyse the organisational and structural factors which shape the operation of African bureaucracies, to locate the principal arenas in which corruption takes place, to identify the major actors involved in corrupt transactions and to outline the main forms and mechanisms by which resources are misused and misappropriated. But setting the scene, identifying the cast and revealing some tricks of the theatrical profession do not, of themselves, explain very much about any particular play. Without some understanding of the plot and the context within which it unfolds, any play is likely to remain incomprehensible.

The earlier discussion linked the growth in corruption to the expansion of government, but no specific conclusions have, as yet, been drawn in regard to the content or objectives of this enhanced role for government. But African governments have purposes and policies and these interact with the factors discussed above and with a range of domestic and external constraints and pressures to produce political environments which are more or less conducive to corruption. Thus, corruption increases not only because African governments do far more than their colonial predecessors, but because of the specific goals they seek to achieve and the means they employ to accomplish them.

Most African economies are open, unbalanced and acutely vulnerable to fluctuations in the world prices of those export commodities which effectively pay for the costs of government. Development programmes and the personal material ambitions of some political leaders depend, in part, on the government's ability to minimise any loss of revenue from the diversion of goods through illicit, untaxed channels. Already weak African economies are weakened further by their inability to extract the maximum revenues from their slender economic bases. One major reason for the shortfall in revenue is widespread and large-scale smuggling. While smuggling itself is not part of what we understand as corruption, it could not take place on its present scale without the collusion of customs officials and other law enforcement agencies.

By volume, much smuggling is in basic commodities which are in chronically short supply. (9) Different economic policies have created different shortages in different countries and many Africans regard it as natural and inevitable to walk across largely invisible and unpatrolled frontiers to get what they need. Thus, for example, Malawians cross into Mozambique to buy maize and rice, while Mozambicans go to Tanzania and Malawi to buy soap, cloth and batteries. Where a state is in economic difficulties, as most African states are, and it is surrounded by other states, the struggle against smuggling is difficult and possibly futile. As a Tanzanian customs officer observes, 'in a land of shortages, no government efforts can effectively curb smuggling - whatever harsh means it uses' (New African, May, 1983, p.16). Thus, in the developed world, smuggling is normally confined to high-priced, highly taxed luxury goods or illicit goods but, in Africa, smuggling extends to commodities of low value in daily use which cross frontiers which are locally perceived as artificial.

Governmental concern at smuggling in basic commodities derives not merely from the anticipated public reaction to shortages, but from the distorting effect it has on patterns of subsidy. In the early 1970s, the military government in Ghana was forced to abolish subsidies on essential goods such as sugar, matchets and tinned meat, not on the usual grounds of escalating cost, but because traders had been buying up the subsidised goods in large quantities and smuggling them into Togo. Smuggling in West Africa sometimes becomes excessively complicated and it has been alleged, for example, that 'Ghana-produced textiles are smuggled into Togo, there to be stamped as of French origin and to be smuggled back into Ghana to enjoy the higher prices commanded by French goods' (West Africa, 19th February, 1973, p.222).

While episodes such as the one described above may have economic consequences and damage inter-governmental relations, they do not often have the financial and political significance of smuggling in gold, drugs, ivory and precious gems. In Sierra Leone, for example, the value of smuggled diamonds is thought to equal or even exceed the value of those legitimately exported. The principal smugglers are thought to be Lebanese or Afro-Lebanese businessmen who apparently no longer find it necessary to use the overland route through Liberia and Guinea, but rather go direct to the national airport and bribe their way through customs (New African, May, 1983, p.12). Sierra Leone is dependent upon a few exports, in particular, alluvial gem diamonds and the illicit mining and smuggling of diamonds has had significant consequences both for the economy and for the political influence of the Lebanese business community. Although the situation in Sierra Leone is serious, it is probably even worse in Zaire. Congo (Brazzaville) appears in the list of the top ten diamond exporting countries, sometimes even ahead of its neighbour, Zaire. This might be less remarkable were it not for the fact that Congo (Brazzaville) has no diamond mines. By the early 1980s, the drain of Zairean revenue had become so serious that, under some Western pressure, the Mobutu government imported a team of Belgian customs officials to help staunch the flow of diamonds out of the country.

Smuggling is intimately connected with the black markets which flourish in so many African countries. It seems that every country has its own term for such markets and their associated profiteering, for example, 'magendo' in Uganda, 'kalabule' in Ghana, 'kamanga' in Angola. Such black markets flourish because few African governments have found it possible to square the economic circle, to match their saving and borrowing and their imports and exports. Most countries have sizeable urban elites whose consumer demands lead to an increase in expensive imports. But the increase in imports is not compensated for by an increase in export revenue, so the familiar response is to mitigate the financial impact of imports by taxing them or imposing quantitative restrictions.

Taxing imports is intended to have the desirable effect of reducing the volume of imports and reducing the loss of foreign exchange in purchasing them but, in practice, the common consequence is to increase smuggling. If taxing and restricting encourages smuggling, not taxing or restricting imports undermines the fragile balance of payments situation. But restrictions on imports not only generates the smuggling of goods into the country, but they may also encourage the smuggling of goods and produce out of the country in order to earn the foreign exchange to pay for the smuggled imports. The delicate vulnerable economies of Africa are thereby doubly damaged in that, in banning or restricting imports, African governments only partly succeed in preventing the outflow of foreign currency while, simultaneously, they are unable to collect any import or export duties on smuggled goods. Where there is a total prohibition on the import of particular goods, such goods naturally command very high prices and the black market can readily absorb the costs of bribing the necessary officials and customs officers.

Smuggling and the corruption associated with it are major problems in a large number of African countries. Just as Congo (Brazzaville) has become a major exporter of diamonds through smuggling from Zaire, Benin has become a large exporter of other countries' cocoa. Governmental concern at the level of smuggling in Nigeria in the late 1970s forced General Obasanjo to appeal to smugglers to make peace with his administration. Instead of issuing dire threats, the Nigerian leader assured the smugglers that 'If they took up farming, Federal and State governments would be ready to give them every assistance' (West Africa, September, 1978, p.37). It is a measure of the problem when smugglers are effectively offered a government re-training programme, but then it is rumoured that during the Shagari administration some Nigerian customs officials had set up a consultancy service to advise trainee smugglers!

Petty smuggling, like petty bribery, excites little sense of public outrage. It has become an established part of the political and economic scene and, as such, it is unlikely to provoke demonstrations or anti-government riots. Public sensitivities to corruption have been somewhat blunted by recent experience and it usually takes something peculiarly grotesque, something on the truly grand scale to ignite popular anger and prompt political action. In recent years, news of such scandals periodically breaks and the consequent political and economic upheavals can be considerable. Corruption on the grand scale is necessarily confined to a few countries and to relatively small groups. When the economy of Nigeria is hundreds of times bigger than, for example, the economy of the Gambia, it is hardly surprising that, in absolute terms, the sums involved in Nigerian corruption scandals often exceed the Gambian total budget. But size is a relative concept and, of course, small countries can be destabilised by scandals involving millions rather than billions.

It is not only the sheer size of the Nigerian economy which facilitates corruption, but the startling pace of oil based economic growth from the late 1960s to the late 1970s. In 1960, agriculture contributed eighty per cent of the value of exports but, twenty years later, it produced only five per cent. During the 1970s, money was literally pouring in and out of government coffers and, between 1967 and 1977, federal revenues increased twenty-two fold. The huge and rapid rise in government income was paralleled by astonishing increases in public expenditure. It is generally against this sort of background that large-scale corruption flourishes and the oil rich, booming Nigeria of the 1970s was an obvious destination for those who were anxious to get a piece of the action and were not too bothered how they acquired it.

Perhaps the most conspicuous example of corruption in Nigeria during the oil boom years was the notorious Cement Scandal of 1975. This example merits closer attention because it graphically illustrates the basic mechanisms of large-scale corruption in Africa. But first it is necessary briefly to set the scene. As I have argued elsewhere 'The priorities of development are not always obvious or consistent and neither are they readily achieved through sudden injections of large sums of money. Like the baby who tries to run before he can walk, any attempt to transform an undeveloped agrarian society almost overnight is bound to produce more than its share of crises and collapses' (Williams in Simmons and Obe, 1983, p.45). Ironically, the Cement Scandal of 1975 was preceded by a period of anxiety about cement supplies. One report suggested that 'it looks like Nigeria will experience a serious cement shortage until at least 1977' (African Development, May, 1974, p.18). If a prediction is going to be wrong, it perhaps might as well be completely wrong.

Rapid economic expansion, particularly in the area of building and infrastructure, almost inevitably produces shortages, bottlenecks and acute problems of financial planning, coordination and control. In 1975, the Nigerian government ordered over twenty million tonnes of cement. Not only was this order some ten times the amount indicated in the Third Development Plan, but it outstripped the cement exporting capacity of Western Europe and the Soviet Union. The sheer scale of the Nigerian order can be gauged by the fact that approximately half the merchant ships in the world which were suitable for carrying cement became involved in supplying Nigeria. This huge quantity was far too much for the port complex at Lagos to handle and, in one estimate, it was 'more than ten times the annual capacity of Apapa, assuming that the docks took nothing other than cement' (African Development, March, 1976, p.271).

Something, it could safely be asserted, had gone wrong. The gross over-ordering of cement suggested either complete incompetence or corruption on a colossal scale. The story of the Cement Scandal is, perhaps unsurprisingly, complicated and technical and important aspects may never be adequately explained (10), but even a bare outline reveals a network and pattern of relationships which have their parallels in other African countries and in a variety of commodity markets.

At this level, corruption rarely consists of the sort of simple, direct transaction between two people that was described in the story at the beginning of this chapter. The object of the exercise is often to make it as difficult as possible for subsequent investigators to identify the culprits or unravel the complex, interlocking arrangements necessary to execute a major financial coup. High level corruption is as much corporate in form as personal and, in the Cement Scandal, 'Dozens of companies specially formed to shoot cement at Nigeria were often created with the connivance of civil servants in a position to lay down the terms of delivery' (African Development, March, 1976, p.271).

To understand the Cement Scandal, it is important to note the way in which external purchasing was organised in Nigeria. It was argued in the preceding chapter that African entrepreneurs have found their niche as intermediaries linking buyers and sellers. The political and economic influence of such entrepreneurs is considerable and hence the purchase of goods and services from abroad is not generally a straightforward bilateral deal. There exist in Africa, and especially Nigeria, vigorous groups of indigenous businessmen and traders who serve as channels or links between government buyers and foreign suppliers. Bilateralism, by definition, tends to exclude such middlemen and thus, in order to protect and further their interests, important intermediaries applied pressure on the Nigerian government to end direct deals between state purchasing agencies and foreign companies.

Large-scale corruption is almost invariably more complex than petty-corruption and there may be several opportunities within a particular scheme to make money. In the Cement Scandal, corruption operated in two stages. The first stage involved the awarding of contracts which, in keeping with the prevailing practice, were placed with Nigerian middlemen acting as agents on behalf of foreign suppliers. In all, eighty one contracts were placed and the contract price was set at fifteen dollars a tonne above the going rate. Naturally, the high contract price was to the mutual personal benefit of those awarding and receiving such contracts, even if it was not a great contribution to the financial stability of Nigeria. The second method of extracting huge profits was in relation to the level of the demurrage rates. (Demurrage is the rate or amount payable per day for failure to unload the cargo of a ship in the agreed time. Time is money and ship owners are entitled to claim compensation for the period when their ships are waiting to discharge their cargoes). In this case, the Ministry of Defence, which was responsible for ordering no less than sixteen million tonnes of cement, agreed to pay demurrage rates which were sixty per cent higher than normal. Thus, not only did government ministries pay inflated prices for enormous quantities of cement they did not need and could not use, but they were also charged excessive demurrage rates when the ports quickly became congested.

The cement contracts were closely investigated and in an official understatement they were described as 'so indefensibly unorthodox that they defied prudence and international usage' (quoted by Turner in Synge (ed), 1977, p.213). If the high contract prices were powerful inducements, the attractions of the demurrage rates were so compelling that some of the ships used were old and unseaworthy. Some were, in fact, on their way to the breakers yard when they were stopped, chartered and loaded for Nigeria. The large discrepancy between the freight costs of such operators and the demurrage compensation paid by the government not only ensured a vast profit, but it provided a powerful incentive to prolong port congestion. The longer the ships carrying cement had to wait off Lagos, the greater the compensation. But because cement must be kept dry and Lagos is one of the world's most humid cities, the longer the wait, the less likely it was that the cement would be of any use when it was eventually landed.

The structure of corrupt arrangements which comprised the Nigerian Cement Scandal produced what has been termed a 'sorcerer's apprentice' effect in that the more cement ordered, the more ships were needed and the more ships chartered, the longer the delays at Lagos and the more demurrage to be paid, the greater the profits. In this way, the scale and costs of the scandal mounted and, by November, 1975, no less than 360 cement ships were queueing off Lagos.

Unlike petty bribery, large scale corruption nearly always involves a number of beneficiaries. The simple bribe in exchange for favoured treatment is frequently replaced by complex conspiracies which sometimes involve unwitting parties. The chain of official, middleman, cement supplier and shipowner or hirer may have one or more corrupt links, but it need not be the case that all the participants are conscious conspirators. In the Nigerian Cement Scandal, the obvious beneficiaries were prominent members of the Ministry of Defence, senior diplomats, high-ranking officials in the Ministries of Housing and Finance, senior army officers and officials of the Central Bank. Outside of government, those who stood to gain were the 'Big Five' Nigerian cement dealers, the ship owners and hirers and the foreign cement suppliers. The official cost of the Cement Racket was put at almost a billion dollars, but many believe that this is a serious underestimate. If the necessary additional expenditure on freight, cement, contract settlements, demurrage, port decongestion equipment and other associated expenses are included, the total cost is probably nearer two billion dollars, or double the official estimate. If the latter figure is more accurate, the Nigerian Cement Scandal accounted for almost a quarter of Nigeria's oil revenue in 1975.

Large-scale corruption normally involves elements of collusion and conspiracy which frequently require the resources and expertise of transnational and foreign companies. Indigenous entrepreneurs and middlemen act as a bridge between corrupt officials and those who aspire to receive or divert government revenue and expenditure. As we have seen, the costs of the Nigerian Cement Scandal were considerable and the economic impact and its attendant publicity contributed to the downfall of the Gowon regime. It might be thought that the Cement Scandal was an aberration, a unique and unparalleled example but, to dispell such misplaced optimism, a brief account of a more recent scandal may be useful.

On February 23rd, 1984, Professor Tam David-West, the Nigerian oil minister, reported that, in the four years of the Shagari administration, Nigeria had lost over sixteen billion dollars in oil income or twenty per cent of the revenue the government should have received from the oil industry. He attributed the loss to a gigantic fraud involving an international 'Mafia' and he warned that his revelations were 'only the tip of an iceberg of corruption in the oil industry' (New African, April, 1984, p.11). Essentially, three kinds of corruption or fraud seemed to have been practised; smuggling, product theft, and evasion of petroleum regulations.

The various smuggling and fraud schemes allegedly involved Nigerians, Asians and European expatriates. The official procedure for selling oil products used in heavy industrial machines and ships' engines was for the Nigerian National Petroleum Corporation (NNPC) to sell at a fixed price of ten kobo per litre to ten authorised dealers and for the dealers to distribute the products to domestic consumers. But, in practice, the oil products were being sold to illegal, unauthorised dealers at fourteen kobo per litre. The unauthorised dealers in turn sold to middlemen with access to jetties and barges. The oil was then pumped on to the barges and sold to the masters of foreign ships in Nigerian waters. The going rate was twenty kobo per litre but the illegal dealers made much more because 'the captains pay in dollars, which are in turn converted into Nigerian currency on the black market at two and a half times the official rate' (New African, April, 1984, p.14).

Oil thefts take many forms but they essentially involve oil destined for one foreign buyer being diverted illegally to another anonymous foreign buyer. According to Professor David-West, no less than 189 tankers had failed to reach the destination listed on their manifests, and the problem was aggravated because 'highly-placed Nigerians sold the oil at inflated prices and money was paid in foreign currency without tax' (West Africa, March 12, 1984, p.581). Illegal exports of gasoline and fuel oil from the

Warri refinery were estimated by the minister to cost up to 400 million dollars each year and he alleged they were organised by some NNPC officials, the corporation's appointed marketing agents, and middlemen representing foreign syndicates.

Clearly, the regulations for selling oil were blatantly and regularly evaded because when a check was made on the seventy two persons who had been granted licences to sell crude oil, it was discovered that only two were active in the oil business and the other seventy had 'sold' their licences. In Nigeria, and in Africa generally, a licence to trade in highly priced commodities is itself a valuable and much sought after piece of property.

The consequences of the various corrupt transactions and frauds in the oil industry were considerable. Not only was there the enormous financial loss running into many billions of dollars, but the illegal diversion of supplies caused serious domestic shortages in oil products. Fuel shortages produced factory closures as well as increased transport costs. Ironically, it was reported, in April, 1984, that 'the Shell Petroleum Development Company Ltd., Nigeria's largest crude oil producer, is unable to send contracted supply boats to Shell offshore installations because of a lack of fuel and oil products' (New African, April, 1984, p.14). The level of fraud and corruption in the oil business generated the fear that, if it continued, Nigeria's oil and other industries might metaphorically, or even literally, grind to a standstill. Obviously, Professor Tam David-West, the Petroleum and Energy Minister, is not perhaps the most objective judge of the misdeeds of the Shagari regime but, even if only some of his allegations against the preceding civilian regime are correct, the scale of corruption in the oil industry was enormous. There is sometimes smoke without fire but, when the clouds of smoke are overwhelming, it is reasonable to assume that a sizeable conflagration is brewing.

Conclusion

This chapter has been concerned to analyse organisational and structural influences on the form and location of corruption and to link these general considerations with an appreciation of the impact made by economic constraints and policy choices. No attempt has been made to present an exhaustive compendium of corrupt practices in Africa partly because of the impossibility of acquiring the requisite information and partly because African ingenuity would soon render it out of date. My purpose has been to outline and illustrate the ways in which corruption commonly works in Africa and to suggest reasons why particular forms and mechanisms are more prevalent than others. To meet these objectives, the analysis has focused particularly on the character of African bureaucracies and on the constraints, pressures and inducements which help determine their roles.

It is not only the case that African bureaucrats are faced with a variety of opportunities and incentives to become corrupt, but that they are subject to immense social, economic and political pressures to conform to group norms and community expectations. Despite the major scandals discussed toward the end of the chapter, it is not the case that most African bureaucrats have Swiss bank accounts. Bureaucratic salaries, even at the lower levels, may seem high in relation to average peasant incomes, but such salaries, together with their corrupt 'emoluments', are often expected to meet high urban living costs and to support members of the official's extended family.

Corruption, as we have seen, serves to refresh the political and administrative parts that legal means cannot reach but, more seriously, it can also clog up those parts so effectively that the machinery of government almost ceases to function in any meaningful sense. Corruption, depending on the circumstances, can act as a lubricant to the engine of state or as sand in the fuel tank. The precise consequences of corruption are always hard to predict and depend on a range of factors including the nature and distribution of political power, the extent of corruption in the system and the objectives or policy goals being sought.

The danger of illustrating only some forms of corruption is that it might be assumed that other, related forms are unimportant or non-existent. But, in the African case, this would be a rash and misleading exercise. In some cases, attempting to curb activities which produce certain kinds of corruption, for example, smuggling, has the effect of generating different forms. If smuggling becomes difficult, some businessmen will be able to achieve their goals through transfer pricing and under or over invoicing. If exchange controls are imposed to restrict the drain of foreign currency, the likely consequence is to produce currency rackets. When a prominent party member or influential businessman wishes to buy something from abroad or deposit funds in external bank accounts, he will pull wires and bribe officials until official exchange control permission is forthcoming. Given the openness of their imbalanced economies, many African states are peculiarly vulnerable to external pressure and manipulation. Given their inadequate resource bases, they face especially difficult domestic problems in promoting economic growth, restraining inflation and re-distributing wealth. Given the best will in the world, 'to issue import licences in such a way as to balance the claims of individual consumers, producers of export crops or manufactured goods, and producers for the home market, within a restricted foreign exchange budget requires infinite finesse and judgement' (West Africa, 8 March, 1976, p.294). Too often, the will, the finesse and the judgement are deficient or the task itself is inherently impossible and, in such circumstances, corruption flourishes.

In the political, administrative and economic conditions which prevail in Africa, when scarcity ensures an excess of demand over supply for public goods, bribery becomes normal rather than deviant. At a different level, a shortage of bed pans gives the same encouragement to bribery as a shortage of public housing or restrictions on foreign currency. But the higher corruption reaches and the larger the sums involved, the more elusive and complex corrupt transactions are likely to be. If large-scale corruption involves complicated collaboration, it is nonetheless the case that, in many instances, an increasingly familiar triangular relationship emerges, not least in the Nigerian cement and oil scandals. The triangle involves collusive partnerships between government and/or parastatal officials, local agents and middlemen, and foreign commercial or governmental interests. In the larger economies, for example, Nigeria, the contractor or supplier may be either indigenous or foreign.

This chapter has been concerned to determine the structural considerations and other general factors which shape the form and incidence of corruption in Africa. But it is clear to the most casual observer that not all African countries endure the same levels of corruption. Zaire and Nigeria may be conspicuously corrupt, but that does not mean that Malawi or Mozambique should be placed in the same category. The next chapter explores the factors which produce different levels of corruption in different societies and, through a short series of illustrative case studies, it draws attention to some of the more distinctive and important patterns of corruption in Africa.

NOTES

(1)   Bienen, 1974, pp.66-130) contains a useful discussion of popular attitudes to members of parliament in Kenya together with a more general analysis of parties, elections and political participation.

(2)   The Watergate episode in the United States suggests that the illegal diversion of excess campaign funds for improper purposes is a problem which extends far beyond Africa.

(3)   Weber's views of bureaucracy are in The Theory of Social and Economic Organisation (1947). The literature discussing Weber's views on bureaucracy is enormous but (Blau and Scott, 1963, pp.30-36) provide a clear, short introduction. For a more sophisticated intellectual portrait, see (Bendix, 1966).

(4)   Problems in maintaining staff records and paying fictitious
        employees are by no means confined to Zaire. In 1984,
        the Kenyan government appointed investigators to find out
        why 85,397 civil servants on the payroll did not appear in
        government records. The head of the civil service, Simon
        Nyachae, is reported as saying that 'he wanted to find
        out whether the people were needed' (The Guardian, 9th
        November, 1984).

(5)   The problem of soldiers extracting tolls is exacerbated by
        the fact that Zairean soldiers are frequently not paid for
        six months at a time. Thus, when Zambians cross into
        Zaire, they find themselves, in effect, paying the soldiers'
        wages. If the bus from the Zambian Copperbelt to the
        Northern Province which passes through Zairean territory
        does not run, the Zairean soldiers go hungry. In such
        circumstances, the soldiers then cross the border and
        commit armed robberies in Zambia (see, M.Ndovi,
        'Zairean Soldiers in Border Racket', New African, May,
        1981, p.41).

(6)   The problem for travellers is that in addition to paying
        bribes to the police, they often have to pay above the
        notional price to get a bus or taxi at all. Taxi owners in
        Ghana and elsewhere demand increasing sums from their
        drivers and the result is 'A lot of drivers complain and
        mention the kalabule (black market) prices of spare parts
        as well as what they have to give to the police. Others
        point out that the car owners have to pay enormous
        amounts to import and clear their cars from ports, added
        costs get passed down until they reach the person in the
        street, who has no one to pass them to' (West Africa, 2nd
        March, 1979, p.577).

(7)   This kind of behaviour is sometimes characterised as
        symptomatic of 'machine' politics and is extensively
        discussed in (Scott, 1972, pp.92-157). But, when the
        notion of 'machine' is applied to Africa, there is always a
        danger of implying that political organisations such as the
        Convention Peoples Party in Ghana enjoyed greater
        substance than they, in practice, possessed.

(8)   The practice of close, trustworthy relatives occupying
        important political positions is not confined to Africa.
        When President Kennedy appointed his brother to be
        Attorney-General of the United States, he did so not
        because of his brother's very brief legal experience, but
        primarily because he could be totally trusted. As
        President Kennedy drily noted, the appointment had the

additional merit of giving his brother some experience before he began practising law.

(9)   Shortages sometimes disappear when elections are imminent.   In the Zambian elections in 1983, 'Some candidates distributed essential commodities that are absent from shop shelves such as washing powder and cooking oil ... Enormous quantities of beer and roast meat were also available so that, for the electorate, October was one long party' (New African, December, 1983, p.21).

(10)   The Cement Scandal remains curiously under-reported and we still depend essentially on the account in (Turner in Synge (ed), 1977, pp.213-223).

5 Patterns of political corruption in Africa

To understand, in general terms, the ways in which corruption works in Africa does not directly illuminate the role it plays in particular countries. Corruption, as we have seen, takes a variety of forms, but specific forms may be the product of more or less uncommon combinations of factors. Most obviously, billion dollar oil frauds are not likely to feature prominently in the corruption scandals of more than a few African states and, where elephant and rhino are scare, corruption associated with the poaching and smuggling of ivory is not likely to be very significant. To labour the point, local conditions shape the form and extent of corruption and for this reason, caution should be exercised in making sweeping judgements about the character and origins of corruption in Africa. To assert in relation to corruption that 'A general phenomenon calls for a general explanation' (Clapham 1985, p.51) seems to assume both that different forms of corruption are attributable to the same cause and that a general explanation is available and desirable. It seems more prudent to recognise the possibility that, given the diversity of political regimes and economic circumstances, corruption of the same type may have different causes or consequences in different contexts. It is also necessary to consider whether, or to what extent, corruption is the outcome of a unique set of circumstances, or derives from the predatory ambitions of individual rulers, rather than from general causes, constraints or pressures.

The notion of a general explanation remains problematic, but the possibility of an explanatory level between the unique and the general remains. It may be that certain forms or levels of corruption are strongly associated with particular regions, types of political regime, degrees of inequality or dependence, rates of economic growth, forms of government and bureaucracy, systems of taxation and trade regulation or specific time periods. But if such an inquiry were launched, the task of collation and comparison would be a daunting one and the final judgement would still be qualitative rather than quantitative.

At first glance, some of these variables offer little promise of progress. If we examine, for example, the location of corruption, most observers would probably argue that the coastal states of West Africa are, and have been, notorious for their corruption, yet Cameroon appears relatively less susceptible. Judgements about the incidence of corruption are bound to be problematic and subject to wide margins of error but, impressionistically, Africa offers some striking contrasts even within particular regions. In East Africa, there has been for many years an obvious contrast between Uganda and Kenya on the one hand and Tanzania on the other. The gap may be diminishing, but it remains true that, for most of the post-independence period Tanzania seemed, by regional standards, relatively free from corruption. In Southern Africa, Malawi seems less corrupt than Zambia, but then so do Mozambique and Zimbabwe.

Such observations illustrate a central problem, to almost any generalisation about the incidence of corruption in Africa, it is possible to find an exception. While corruption may be low in the pro-western autocracy of Dr. Hastings Banda in Malawi, it is extremely high in other pro-western autocracies. If corruption is low in Marxist Mozambique and socialist Tanzania, it is relatively high in humanist Zambia. Such differences are not readily subsumed under any general explanation unless it be one that is extremely vague and possibly vacuous.

If there is less corruption in Ghana under Rawlings than there was under Limann or Acheampong, there may still be more than there was under the once notorious regime of Kwame Nkrumah. Our perceptions of the level of corruption are influenced not merely by comparative judgements of other countries, but by comparisons over time. The Nkrumah regime seemed particularly corrupt because we had, at that time, few points of reference. By the standards of his successors, the extensive inquiries into Nkrumah's personal transactions now seem excessive, almost ludicrous. (1) The personal wealth of modern African leaders is now often a cause for self-congratulation rather than concealment. In 1957, Nkrumah offered a bet to Felix Houphouet-Boigny of the

Ivory Coast concerning the relative development of their respective countries over the next ten years. Nkrumah was overthrown in 1966 and he and his regime have since been considerably discredited. Houphouet-Boigny, on the other hand, admits that he has a fortune deposited in Swiss banks and argues, with some audacity, that he has invested a great deal of his wealth in the Ivory Coast as 'proof of his confidence in the country' (Africa Now, July, 1983, p. 22).

This suggests that rather than present a photographic snapshot of a number of African countries at any one moment in time, it may be more illuminating to examine how and in what forms corruption develops within particular societies over time. The choice of illustrative case studies is made difficult, partly because of the limited knowledge of the author and partly because of a desire not to replicate existing book length analyses. On the former ground and with some regret, the former French colonies have been excluded and, on the latter grounds, Zaire and Ghana have been eliminated. Taking size and geographic balance into consideration, Nigeria, Kenya and Zambia were selected, but the fourth choice has posed intractable problems primarily because of my desire to include some discussion of Afro-Marxist or Afrocommunist regimes. Unfortunately, Mozambique and Angola, the leading contenders in terms of comparable size are and have been ravaged by civil war and external subversion and their comparability with the other cases may be in doubt. The inadequate solution to my difficulty is to treat Afro-Marxist regimes as a group and to emphasise what it is they have in common which has a particular bearing on the form and incidence of corruption. This is an unsatisfactory compromise, but it is perhaps preferable to excluding altogether consideration of the almost twenty per cent of African states that have adopted Afro-Marxism as a self-definition. (2)

It may be objected that the levels of corruption in Nigeria, Kenya and Zambia are high, but the force of the objection depends on what is counted as average. If Nigeria has sometimes seemed to rival Zaire as the most corrupt country in Africa, Kenya and especially Zambia appear more representative of the state of affairs prevailing in much of tropical Africa, including the former French colonies. The omission of Zaire and Ghana is not intended as an unreserved endorsement of the judgements of Gould (1979) or Le Vine (1975). In both cases, though in very different ways, the authors invaluable and illuminating investigations are presented in unhelpful and inadequate explanatory frameworks. They seem to illustrate a common desire to impose shape on the amorphous and inject order into chaos. This is not to say that corruption entirely resists the explanatory ambitions of either a mechanical Marxism or American political science qua science, but suggests that conceptual schemes should be constructed to fit the evidence, not imposed on it.

In the illustrative case studies which follow, an effort is made to identify the forces shaping the growth, character and significance of corruption in a variety of settings. When this task is completed, it should be possible to assess whether, or how much, the general constraints and pressures which encourage corruption in Africa are modified, exacerbated or resisted by the particular circumstances and experiences of individual countries. From this analysis, we will be better placed to detect whether there are any obvious patterns of political corruption in Africa and to test the utility of any likely general explanations.

A. Kenya, Corruption And Kenyatta.

In 1984, a major public inquiry was conducted into the activities of Charles Njonjo, the former Kenyan Minister of Constitutional Affairs and Attorney-General. During the inquiry, it was alleged that Njonjo had been implicated in a variety of dubious and improper activities including arms smuggling, the sale of work permits, illegal currency deals and the diversion of election funds for private use. The inquiry was not a trial, but it served to damage and discredit politically Njonjo and a number of his highly placed supporters including three former cabinet ministers, four assistant ministers and some prominent backbench MPs.

But it should not be assumed that Njonjo and his supporters were the only rotten apples in the Kenyan barrel. If the Njonjo inquiry was Kenya's Watergate, Njonjo himself was a much more powerful version of J.Edgar Hoover. Like Hoover, he was believed to have used his position as Attorney-General to collect useful 'information' about his political associates and opponents. Such information made him both dangerous and seemingly indispensable to Kenya's political leadership. But Njonjo was vastly more important than Hoover ever was because he had powerful political supporters in the Cabinet and in the National Assembly and because he enjoyed the support and confidence of the governments of Israel, South Africa and Malawi. (3) In short, Njonjo was seen as a threat to the leadership of President Daniel arap Moi and it was further believed that Njonjo was actively plotting to seize control of the government. In such circumstances, Njonjo had to be discredited in such a way that his political threat was defused while his sensitive information remained secret. Many of the charges which produced the downfall of Njonjo involved corruption, but his real crime was overreaching ambition. Corruption alone has rarely been seen as a justification for removing senior members of the Kenyan government.

The activities of Njonjo and leading supporters like Stanley

Oloitiptip are not isolated examples of unusual deviance in the conduct of public office in Kenya, but rather stem from a particular political context and history. The major aspects of contemporary Kenyan politics can be seen to derive largely from the colonial experience and its repercussions because as a settler colony, a 'white man's country', Kenya experienced in an acute form the impact of colonial rule. It received larger investments than non-settler colonies and, from the completion of the Mombasa to Lake Victoria railway in 1901, it was anticipated that the Kenyan economy would generate sufficient revenues to meet not only colonial administrative costs, but also repay the loans for infrastructure development.

White farming was subsidised and promoted, while many Africans were deprived of their land and 'encouraged' to work for Europeans. The persuasion took a variety of forms and was achieved 'partly by force, partly by taxation, and partly by preventing them (Africans) from having access to enough land or profitable crops to enable them to pay taxes without working for wages' (Leys, 1974, p.30). As a result, more and more Africans were forced into wage employment and, by the mid-1920s, over half the Kikuyu and Luo men worked for Europeans. The Kikuyu were in a pivotal position in a geographical, political and economic sense because they were the group most directly influenced by the policies and priorities of white rule. In consequence, they 'had unusual access to the meaning of racist discrimination on one side and to modernising influences on the other' (Davidson, 1978, p. 263). They enjoyed the greatest access to educational and other opportunities while, at the same time, they felt most acutely the alienation of their land.

In such a context, it was only to be anticipated that the Kikuyu would play a central role in the earliest stirrings of nationalism in Kenya and that they would later feature so prominently in the so-called 'Mau Mau' Emergency in the early 1950s. (4) The 'Mau Mau' disturbances revealed graphically not only growing anti-colonial sentiment, but increasing economic divisions within the Kikuyu. In this sense, 'Mau Mau' was as much a civil war as a colonial rebellion and the defeat of the forest fighters had profound consequences for the values and character of the first independent Kenyan government. The forest fighters or 'terrorists' were recruited overwhelmingly from the ranks of the uneducated, unemployed and landless Kikuyu and their defeat was a victory, not just for the colonial security forces, but for the 'loyalists', the educated, employed, materially ambitious Kikuyu.

Kenyatta, Kenya's first president, was detained by the British authorities and, in somewhat dubious circumstances, found guilty of being one of the organisers of 'Mau Mau'. His reputation, as a 'leader of darkness and death', soon became well established in the popular consciousness of whites. In view of Kenyatta's later status as the epitome of moderation and 'responsible' African leadership, there is a certain irony attached to the entire episode. But there is something more than irony in the charge that Kenyatta, far from being a prime mover in the disturbances was, in fact, on the 'Mau Mau' death list. From this perspective, Kenyatta's detention by the British is viewed as 'a form of protective custody' (anonymous Kenyan authors, 1982, p.23).

Over time, the Kenyan economy was seen to be dominated by the foreign owned plantations and ranches, together with the settler owned mixed farms, and these enterprises were widely perceived as paragons of agricultural efficiency and productivity. The importance of this sector was firmly established in the minds of the emergent African political elite and Kenyatta was emphatic, from the time of his release from detention in 1961, that the rights of private property were to be respected, that settlers should be persuaded to stay and that business and foreign investment were to be encouraged. In the period immediately preceding independence, the more enlightened settlers argued that it was important to encourage the advancement of a strata of Africans who would share the aspirations, values and economic interests of Europeans. In Kenyatta and some of his associates in the Kenya African National Union (KANU), they found willing collaborators. Once the inevitability of independence was accepted, it became imperative for the settler community and foreign capital to ensure that the transfer of political power did not entail any fundamental social or economic change. The new African leadership under Kenyatta had a similar and compatible interest in inheriting political power and its associated economic opportunities.

The land hunger of Kenyans, and especially the Kikuyu, had been partly assuaged by the Swynnerton Plan of the 1950s and partly by arrangements made as part of the independence settlement. (5) These reforms left large areas of prime land under foreign or settler control but, in granting some African peasant farmers access to credit and land they gave a significant stimulus to petty rural capitalism in Kikuyu country. In so doing, they appeased the land demands of the more affluent and more vocal at the price of exacerbating political and economic divisions with the African population. (6)

From independence, the style, tone and strategy of the Kenyan government has been clear. Western opinion began to change because, despite the early fear of the KANU leadership, it was soon apparent that it was as committed to the ethos of private enterprise as the foreign investors and settler community. In practice, Kenya's political leaders have sometimes appeared as active in business and farming as they have been in politics.

Indeed, substantial personal wealth, however acquired, seems to be a condition of success in Kenyan politics. Even radical critics of Kenyatta and his policies, men like Oginga Odinga and J.M. Kariuki were 'big men', men of considerable substance and extensive commercial interests. Given the conspicuous interweaving of business and political careers, it became increasingly difficult to separate private and public purposes.

By 1965, the strategy of the Kenyan government could be identified as one of the co-option or harassment of political opponents, the pursuit of a capitalist road to development and the progressive enrichment of the political and bureaucratic elite. The standard joke of the late 1960s concerned the discovery of a new ethnic grouping, the Wabenzi, whose main distinguishing feature was the possession of one or more Mercedes Benz motor cars. The joke reflected the contemporary preoccupation with conspicuous consumption and the popular association of politicians with self-aggrandizement.

Almost inevitably, rumours and stories began to circulate both about the size of some personal fortunes and about the methods used to acquire them. Kenyatta, the father of the nation, almost took on the mantle of a monarch. When Kenyatta moved between State House in Nairobi and his homes in Gatundu, Mombasa and Nakuru, it was less the seat of government that moved, so much as an entire court. Kenyatta became the centre of governmental activity and thus access to him was the sine qua non of preferment for politicians, bureaucrats and businessmen alike. As discussed earlier, access to decision-makers is never unlimited and not always free in Africa. The court 'gatekeepers' in Kenya extracted sizeable entry fees and most visitors left with lighter wallets or thinner cheque books after having 'voluntarily' contributed to one of Kenyatta's favourite causes or schemes.

Since independence, Kenya's political institutions have atrophied. The government had no need of a mass party after independence because it feared rather than desired the political mobilisation of the masses. The consequence was that KANU degenerated into little more than an arena 'where political bosses of rival factions collided and colluded in their perennial struggle for the power and patronage of party, governmental and parastatal offices' (Jackson and Rosberg, 1982, p. 103). KANU is now the only political party in Kenya, but it is no more than a hollow shell.

The National Assembly has resisted to some degree the atrophy which has all but destroyed KANU, but its role is decidedly limited in regard to governmental strategy or the major issues of public policy. Members of the National Assembly are free to acquire extra income from any source without restriction and without need for disclosure. They receive very favourable treatment in regard to loans and mortgages and many hold some extra-parliamentary appointments. The inducement of such appointments has proved effective in silencing actual or potential parliamentary critics of the government.

Members of Parliament act as spokesmen or agents for their constituents and they see their role as lobbyists to obtain extra resources and services for their constituents. Indeed, part of their enthusiastic acquisition of extra income is attributable to their need to help 'finance, or at least provide seed money for the projects in which they are involved' (Barkan (ed), 1979, p. 74). Clearly, not all MPs are able to deliver resources and services all the time and the failure of MPs and ministers to meet the expectations of their constituents leads to electoral defeat. When resources are in scarce supply, political upheavals occur as, for example, when almost half the incumbents were defeated in 1979. It is this tension between the need to deliver constituency services with only limited access to finite resources that produces the high turnover in elections and the illusion of change in Kenyan politics.

Just as the National Assembly provides a safety valve for popular discontent, the electoral process regulates entry into, and advancement within, the political elite as well as serving to renew regime legitimacy. But neither the National Assembly nor the electoral process are intended or permitted to change the central thrust of the government's policies. M.Ps are expected to remain content that their positions give them income, status, access to credit and patronage, and the possibility of preferment.

Local politicians and officials tend to share the business philosophy of their national counterparts. One consequence is that the implementation of national public policies is subject to the distorting effects of corruption and clientelism. A study of housing policy in Nairobi (Temple and Temple in Grindle (ed), 1980, pp 224-249) shows clearly the considerable discrepancy between officially stated policy preferences and actual performance. Despite an official commitment to the provision of low cost housing in the 1960s, housing resources were, in practice mainly directed to the needs of the better-off residents of Nairobi. An important factor contributing to the failure to provide adequate low-cost housing was that the city councillors 'were by and large an upwardly mobile group who shared the middle-class consumption aspirations of Nairobi's elite, and benefited politically from allocating council housing to other members of this elite' (Temple and Temple in Grindle (ed), 1980, p. 238). Personal contacts and influence seem to be the keys to unlocking scare housing resources and the informal social networks of Nairobi's more affluent residents were easily able to circumvent formal bureaucratic allocation procedures. In such contexts, there is often no need to resort to unvarnished bribery or extortion because of the shared appreciation of mutually beneficial social networks and interactions. Thus, the direct immediate exchange of specific favours is replaced by indirect, deferred, unspecified understandings.

The allocation of scarce housing resources provides not only an opportunity to extend networks of potentially valuable contacts, but a unique chance to reward supporters, relatives and friends. To those with adequate accommodation, public housing is a means to extra income through sub-letting. Given the disparity between market and council rents, illegal sub-letting is almost a licence to print money and this creates considerable incentives to acquire, by illicit means, as many units of public housing as possible. With commendable restraint, the authors of the Nairobi study observe that 'It is not unknown for influential individuals to secure public housing in more than one city in Kenya' (Temple and Temple in Grindle (ed), 1980, p.247). The principal beneficiaries of the bias in housing allocation are often civil servants or local government officials who already enjoy preferential treatment in regard to bank loans and mortgages. The purchase or other acquisition of property for rent is seen as a guaranteed and far from time consuming method of making substantial sums of money and officials have been keen to exploit their status and contacts.

Civil servants have long been a favoured economic group in Kenya and, traditionally, they have enjoyed much higher salaries than their equivalents in, for example, neighbouring Tanzania. More importantly, there is no Kenyan equivalent of the Tanzanian leadership code which attempts to limit the availability of additional sources of income to politicians and civil servants. On the contrary, the extra-curricular activities of the Kenyan bureaucracy have received the official blessing of a government commission which asserted 'there ought in theory to be no objection to the ownership of property or involvement in business by members of the public services to a point where their wealth is augmented perhaps substantially by such activities' (Ndegwa, 1971, p.14). As a consequence, it is hardly surprising that the bureaucracy was popularly regarded less as 'an instrument for the pursuit of public policy as it was an avenue of promoting private ambitions and interests' (Barkan (ed), 1979, p.105).

If Kenyatta and members of his family were strongly rumoured to have acquired considerable fortunes through the use and abuse of public office, the successor regime headed by Daniel arap Moi has hardly been able to escape being labelled in a similar fashion. If members of the Kenyatta family were thought to have been involved in the illegal export of ivory to the Middle East and Hong Kong, a recent study alleges that, in the Moi government, 'kickbacks', graft and conflict of interests are evident at all levels' (anonymous Kenyan authors, 1982, p. 47). The same study asserts that the regime is plagued by large-scale corruption and fraud involving ivory, gemstones, maize, land speculation, the funding of co-operatives, the appointment of ministerial relatives to the boards of multinational companies and the mismanagement of parastatals (anonymous Kenyan authors, 1982, pp 101-114). In short, neither the brief period of uncertainty after Kenyatta's death nor the fall of Njonjo are indications of a clash of values or ideology, but rather reflect a scramble for power. The replacement of Kenyatta by Moi is less a confirmation of the much vaunted political stability of Kenya as a changing of faces at the top, a change of personalities rather than policies. If and when policies are adopted which threaten the vested interests of the political, bureaucratic and commercial elites, the stability of Kenya will be properly put to the test. Meanwhile, as far as many Kenyan political entrepreneurs are concerned, it is a case of 'business as usual'.

B. Corruption in Zambia

In October 1983, Dr. Kenneth Kaunda was re-elected as President of Zambia, a post he has held since independence in 1964. At the formal oath swearing ceremony, Kaunda took the opportunity of rebuking members of the Zambian National Assembly for making wild and unsubstantiated allegations of corruption in the United National Independence Party (UNIP) and in the government. If MPs persisted in making such charges, Kaunda warned they would be 'dis-elected' and removed from the National Assembly. Earlier in 1983, the MP for Ndola, Roy Rodgers Chaiwa, was removed on similar grounds and was not allowed to contest his seat at the subsequent election. President Kaunda insisted that 'if any Member of Parliament has any evidence of corruption, let him go to the Anti-Corruption Commission or produce evidence before the House' (Africa, November, 1983, p. 31).

Kaunda's concern at the damage done to the reputation of the government and UNIP by false accusations of corruption was matched by his equally public concern about the need to implement a 'house cleaning' operation to sort out corrupt officials and ministers. To further this end, he proposed strengthening and extending the Leadership Code of Conduct and acting on the findings of the Anti-Corruption Commission. Significantly, in appointing a new Cabinet in November, 1983, Kaunda dropped only one minister, Mufaya Mumbuna, from the previous Cabinet. A month later, Mumbuna appeared before a Lusaka court to answer charges that he had accepted a luxury car in exchange for granting a mining licence to a foreign firm (New Africa, February, 1984, p.23). Kaunda's concern about corruption and misconduct in UNIP and in the government as a whole has long been a matter of public record and it is the case that individuals convicted of corruption have suffered severe penalties. But punishing individuals and warning their colleagues does not afford any clear insight into the place of corruption in Zambians government and politics. To understand the role of corruption, we need to look at the factors which have shaped the Zambian polity and the policies pursued by Kaunda's government.

Kaunda's first government was formed from his party, UNIP, which had led the drive for independence. But his nationalist party was not as cohesive and disciplined as Kaunda might have wished. One problem was that 'the unevenness of the nationalist impact, as well as the short-duration of the anti-colonial struggle within a culturally and linguistically fragmented society, meant that the unity which UNIP established was fragile' (Tordoff (ed), 1974, p.10). Once the colonial enemy had been defeated, it was only to be anticipated that different regions and factions would vigorously compete for their rightful share of the country's limited economic resources.

Political independence had been won at the negotiating table, rather than on the battlefield and, by implication, the machinery of the colonial state was inherited in a modified form rather than destroyed or transformed. UNIP had not espoused any clear or comprehensive view of the new, independent Zambia and the relatively smooth transfer of power seemed to suggest that Kaunda and his associates were not regarded as dangerous radicals. (7) Independence came relatively quickly and certainly without the need to develop a revolutionary cadre to mobilise the rural population into taking up armed struggle. (8)

Independence produced almost irresistable demands for a range of social and economic benefits. In the short-term, the high copper prices of the immediate post-independence years enabled the government to accede to such pressures and, in particular, the standard of living of the urban working class improved appreciably. In addition to the general expectation of improved government services and benefits, some groups had specific claims which were particularly hard not to recognise. The party activists who had worked hardest for independence expected their just reward and, in consequence, 'Access to loans, licenses, employment opportunities and the early emphasis on agricultural co-operatives favoured local U.N.I.P. officials and strong U.N.I.P. regions' (Gertzel (ed), 1984, p.5).

The initial government responses to independence produced problematic consequences which helped encourage the spread of corruption. While the first National Development Plan gave high priority to investment in education, the investment was predicated on the expectation of a substantial expansion and diversification of employment opportunities which has yet to take place. The production of large numbers of educated young people with aspirations to white-collar employment has served to intensify greatly the scramble for jobs in the public sector. The reality is that Zambia's economy is as dependent on copper now as it was at independence. In its share of exports by value, copper had increased from 90% in 1965 to 92% in 1978 (Southall, 1980, p.94).

After independence, the character of UNIP began to change. The struggle for independence had been won and many of the victors left party posts for governmental, bureaucratic, parastatal or multi-national employment. In this last respect, the potential advantages of employing in senior positions Africans with good political connections were quickly appreciated by most of the foreign companies operating in Zambia. In some cases, the apparent lack of substantive responsibilities entrusted to such 'political' appointees was a good indication that their tasks were of an essentially liaising or facilitating kind. They often proved particularly valuable in sensitive matters such as arranging unusual departures from stated policies in areas such as securing import permits, ensuring the availability of scare foreign exchange and remitting profits and expatriate salaries.

The organisation and vitality of UNIP declined for other reasons as well as the departure of many of its leading lights to public and private sector posts. In the 1960s, there were frequent instances of local party officials misusing and misappropriating party funds and central party officials did not always find it easy to control or regulate such excesses. After the introduction of a one-party state in 1972, the competitive element disappeared and the need for party recruitment seemed less pressing. (9) In order to reduce the level of fraud and inadequate accounting, local officials were prohibited from keeping any of the funds they collected and, as a result, subscription revenues fell sharply. In consequence, 'The tension between central and local officials over political money which had existed prior to 1973 was overcome at the expense of a viable local-level party organisation' (Scott, 1982, p.410). Thus potentially greater financial probity and efficiency was purchased at the price of local organisational decay.

By 1968, it seemed that the fruits of the independence victory had all been consumed. The Zambianisation and expansion of the bureaucracy had gone as far, if not further, than financial constraints allowed and, therefore, the Kaunda government was starved of the kinds of resources necessary to maintain and develop political support. But the economic reforms of 1968-1970 opened up new possibilities through the expansion of the parastatal sector and the encouragement of indigenous private enterprise. Although not publicly justified in such terms, the major significance of the reforms 'was precisely that, by extending government's control and influence, it gave new leeway for patronage and sharing of benefits' (Southall, 1980, p.97).

The principal beneficiaries of the encouragement to private enterprise were often those who already enjoyed senior positions in the public or parastatal sectors. Public office and the status, contacts and salaries that go with it facilitate the accumulation of capital for private business ventures. Such accumulation can, of course, be accelerated where officials accept or solicit additional remuneration in the form of bribes. In the early 1970s, 'a number of officials (including two permanent secretaries) were prosecuted on a variety of charges relating to the sale of citizenship for cash, furniture, electrical equipment and even motor vehicles' (Baylies and Szeftel, 1982, p. 198). In the agricultural sectors, both the co-operative movement and the loan schemes for farmers were controlled by UNIP officials and they were mainly organised and distributed for the benefit of an already favoured group of party members and supporters. In the parastatal sector, the lack of coherent policy and adequate standards of accountability encouraged speculation and rumours about widespread corruption and mismanagement. (10) As the values and attitudes of private enterprise have received governmental blessing, the consequence, in one scholar's view, is that 'the sense of national commitment is displaced by individual careerism' (Turok, 1981, p.433). If Turok has a somewhat optimistic view about pre-reform levels of 'national commitment', he is surely right to observe that, in the parastatal sector, 'senior executives and managers have contrived to gain additional privileges .. (and) to enrich themselves in dubious ways' (Turok, 1981, p.433).

If it is obvious that UNIP is and has been a party of patronage, (11) it is equally certain that increasingly the distinction between patronage and corruption, between cementing political loyalities and acquiring purely personal gains, has become almost irretrivably blurred. In the past ten years, there have been a number of major scandals which have implicated former holders of the most important public positions including government ministers, senior party officials, a governor of the Bank of Zambia, a Commissioner of Police, the Commander of the Zambian Air Force, and the Chief Paymaster of the Defence Forces (Africa Contemporary Record, 1976-1977, p.B406; Africa Contemporary Record 1978-1979 p.b.453).

The response of the political leadership to the growth of corruption in Zambia is not without its ironies and anomalies. Like Tanzania, Zambia has adopted a Leadership Code, but there appear to be only a couple of cases where individuals have formally divested themselves of business interests in compliance with the Code (Baylies and Szeftel, 1982, p. 204) and prosecutions for violations of the Leadership Code have been largely conspicuous by their absence. While President Kaunda has maintained his personal reputation for incorruptability, he seems unable or unwilling to curb the more dubious activities of some of his colleagues and associates. If heads have metaphorically rolled when corrupt politicians and officials have been uncovered, this does not seem to have prevented the hydra of corruption from quickly re-appearing.

At a deeper level, there appears to be some basic inconsistency in Kaunda's economic strategy and its consequences for corruption. Having enacted reforms both to ensure that the parastatals function on a more commercial basis and to promote the growth of an indigenous business class, Kaunda has, nevertheless, been quoted as saying that 'the fight against capitalist tendencies was a big problem' (Africa Contemporary Record, 1976-1977, p. B406). In Zambia, as elsewhere in Africa, corruption can best be understood within a particular political and economic framework and the condemnation of corruption by those who help to create and sustain such a framework addresses the symptom rather than the underlying condition. The institutionalisation of party patronage in Zambia has promoted sectional, factional or individual interests above any notion of the public or national interest and, in such a context, the party slogan, 'It Pays to Belong to UNIP' is increasingly likely to be taken literally.

C. Afro-Marxist Regimes and Corruption

The so-called 'Afro-Marxist' or 'Afrocommunist' states do not form a monolithic and undifferentiated bloc. If they articulate their goals in a more or less common jargon, they nevertheless derive from a variety of political roots and confront environments of differing complexity and hostility. But their commitment to some form of Marxist-Leninism, to 'scientific' rather than 'African' socialism, to the notion of a vanguard rather than mass party and their insistence on the revolutionary primacy of the working class suggests that there is some merit in treating them as a distinctive group of states. This is not to deny that the use of labels such as 'Afro-Marxist' may imply a degree of homogeneity that does not actually exist, but rather to emphasise that, in terms of ideological outlook, policy priorities and organisational characteristics, these states are significantly different from their African neighbours.

The major Afro-Marxist states, Mozambique, Angola and Ethiopia, pose particular analytical problems both because they have only recently come into existence and because, for most of their brief revolutionary histories, they have been ravaged by civil war and a variety of natural calamities. It is therefore premature to make any firm judgements about the levels or patterns of corruption likely to arise in such regimes. No major Afro-Marxist state has enjoyed a prolonged period of respite from the dislocations and distortions of war and, in such circumstances, policy achievements are unlikely to match rhetorical claims and aspirations. Where field research conditions are impossible, it may be tempting to give greater credence to government propaganda and the reports of ideological sympathisers than is perhaps justified. (12) No Afro-Marxist regime has yet been able to realise its political and economic ambitions and, in practice 'the dream of the command socialist economy is far removed from the reality of the desparately improvised crisis-management state' (Young 1982, p. 30).

Given their relatively small scale and extreme state of underdevelopment, it was never likely that the Soviet Union would provide a useful role model for the Afro-Marxist states. Their precarious economic circumstances and paucity of resources have ensured that, for the most part, they remain critically dependent upon Western trade, technology, personnel and investment. In these respects, Afro-Marxist states are sometimes difficult to distinguish from their 'capitalist' neighbours, for example, Congo-Brazzaville has remained, like other former French colonies, within the franc zone and solicits French and other foreign investment. Similarly, economic necessity ensures that Angola maintains its dependence on the international oil corporations who contribute so much to her govenment's revenues. In Mozambique, a combination of military and economic pressures impelled Samora Machel into signing the Nkomati Accord with the arch-enemy, South Africa. In short, the Afro-Marxist regimes have had to compromise to survive. Their economi- and political waters are so turbulent that keeping afloat has become the major preoccupation. The consequence of the continuing and deepening dependence and disruption is that it becomes increasingly difficult to identify any particular economic or political development as a distinctive product of Afro-Marxism.

Despite the confusion and the constraints, it is possible to grasp the central goals of these regimes even if the obstacles to their fulfilment currently seem insuperable. Afro-Marxist regimes seek to create new political and economic systems intended to solve the problems of production and distribution. The goal is both to avoid the uneven growth characteristic of the 'capitalist' states like Nigeria, Kenya, or the Ivory Coast and to overcome the negative growth of 'socialist' states like Tanzania. To all shades of Afro-Marxist, the common enemy is capitalism and its attendant social and economic consequences. The struggle against capitalism and its social products can take a variety of forms, for example, where an indigenous ruling class existed, as in Ethiopia, the task is one of expropriating or eliminating it. But where no national bourgeoisie was allowed or encouraged to develop before independence, the struggle has been directed at preventing its subsequent emergence.

Afro-Marxist governments tend to see corruption as a pernicious legacy or attribute of capitalism and colonialism. (13) In particular, they construe the actions of the departing colonial powers as exacerbating the problems of independence. In the transitional period prior to independence in Mozambique, the Portugese authorities conceded extravagant wage claims to many workers. To the new ruling party, the Frente de Libertacao de Mozambique (FRELIMO), the increases were awarded both because the Portugese would not be around for the financial reckoning and to fuel unrealistic acquisition urges among the workers. The party's conclusion was that 'The roots of indiscipline, liberalism and corruption ... can be traced to the capitalist strategy during the collapse of colonial rule' (quoted in Ottaway, 1981, p.75). Corruption is identified as a peculiarity of capitalism which, by implication, will disappear as and when capitalism disappears and workers and peasants are released or re-educated from their petty bourgeois aspirations.

But the governments of Mozambique and Angola have been unable to establish or maintain consistent control over the territories of their states. The Angolan government has faced not just one, but two rebel organisations backed by foreign powers. In Mozambique, the security situation had deteriorated by 1985 almost to Angolan proportions. These governments are involved in a bloody struggle for survival and their resources are often inadequate to discharge the first function of government, the maintenance of civil order. Yet, in the midst of war and chaos, these regimes strive to transform political and economic institutions and attitudes. In the best of circumstances, such a transformation would be a formidable undertaking requiring 'intensive, direct, continuous and relatively efficient administration and control'. (Callaghy in Rosberg and Callaghy (eds), 1979, p. 114). In reality, the military and economic situations, the destabilisation policies of South Africa and the acute shortages of educated and motivated manpower combine to ensure that government performance is limited, sporadic and often ineffective. Governments which are unable to discharge their law and order functions seem unlikely to achieve their wider ambitions.

Nevertheless, Afro-Marxist regimes sometimes pursue their goals irrespective of unfavourable circumstances. The Ethiopian regime having brutally purged its class enemies and political rivals undertook a policy of agricultural collectivisation. It seemed, at least in the short run, that some sacrifice in production was entailed by this collectivisation, but it was deemed necessary 'to head off the formation of a kulak class which would in turn give rise to "petty bourgeois" individualism undermining socialism' (Ottaway, 1981, p. 196). Similarly, both Mozambique and Angola initially sought to replace Portugese plantations and estates with state farms rather than encourage more peasant farming. Such policies may be pursued partly because of a belief in the greater efficiency of larger units, but it is also consistent with inhibiting the formation of potentially antagonistic social classes.

The major governmental implication of the hostility to capitalism, and to associated tendencies like corruption, is to place an even larger burden on the public sector than is generally the case in Africa. The public sector has become the designated mechanism for organising and controlling production, distribution and exchange at the same time that most of its skilled and experienced managers and officials fled or were purged. In the absence of a market system, the planning and organisation of production and distribution is a labour intensive and complex affair which even developed nations, such as the Soviet Union, frequently find extremely difficult. To attempt the task in an underdeveloped state ravaged by civil war suggests an unusual degree of faith or optimism. In practice, petty trading has proved virtually impossible to control and it is hardly surprising that, in Mozambique, it was found necessary to permit some of the 'people's shops' to return to private management.

Thus, the creation of Afro-Marxist states brought about a major growth in the state and parastatal bureaucracies together with an expanded set of responsibilities. The departure of the Portugese and their collaborators left an administrative and managerial vacuum in Angola and Mozambique. Those with proven experience and skills were seen as agents of the colonial regime and therefore not to be trusted. The struggle against the affluent educated elite, against bourgeois tendencies, and against internal 'enemies', served to 'put a powerful weapon in the hands of the untalented and unscrupulous for whom self-advancement has lain in taking the hard line' (White, 1985, p.330). This combination of developments has encouraged the emergence of overblown, underqualified and often unproductive bureaucracies which have drained state resources rather than acted as engines of socialist development. The abysmal performance of the public sector in Congo-Brazzaville moved its leader to observe that 'corruption and embezzlement have reached disquieting proportions' (Africa Contemporary Record 1976-77,B.493).

The acquisitive urges of state employees have proved generally difficult to restrain and the inability of governments to meet the basic needs of their peoples encourages the growth of competing authority structures and alternative economic mechanisms. In practice, this means both increased support for rebel organisations which, with external support, are able to supply goods otherwise in short supply and the growing displacement of government shops and distribution systems by an expanding and dominant black market. In a civil war, economic sabotage can be more effective and less risky than a military offensive and, in Angola, concerted efforts have been made through smuggling and associated corruption to undermine the fragile economic position of the MPLA government.

While smuggling can involve basic necessities as well as luxury goods, it normally only involves corruption where expensive items are concerned. In 1984, a large corruption trial was held in Luanda which centred on the destabilising influence of the kamanguistas, the illicit dealers in diamonds. The prosecutor assessed the financial losses to the government caused by the diamond rackets at $96 million annually in the years 1981 to 1983. Throughout the corruption trial, the economic sabotage of the rebels and their foreign backers was stressed and the government seemed to be trying to demonstrate that, while corruption was an integral part of government in neighbouring Zaire, it was a manifestation of attempted destabilisation in Angola. While the survival of the MPLA regime is, with continued Cuban support, not immediately in doubt, the prospects for an end to capitalism and corruption in the context of continuing civil war and economic sabotage are not encouraging.

If Afro-Marxist states vary considerably in scale, political coherence and economic viability, many observers have identified Mozambique as the most important experiment in this form of regime. But judgements on African politics are notoriously uncertain and Crawford Young's assessment that Mozambique possesses 'a sophisticated and united leadership; a relatively clear-cut ideological identity; a coherent political underpinning in FRELIMO' (Young, 1982, p. 96) has somewhat been overtaken by the deteriorating security situation and the increasing difficulty the Machel government has in enforcing its will outside of Maputo.

If there is a serious question mark over the future of Afro-Marxism in southern Africa, it is clear that, compared to most of their neighbours, the Afro-Marxist states are not characterised by high levels of corruption. (14) But equally clearly, it is possible to assert that they have not eradicated corruption and nor are they likely to in the economic and political conditions which currently prevail. Compared to many of its neighbours, Mozambique takes the issue of corruption very seriously and responds to alleged cases with severity and without much regard for Western notions of legal procedure. In 1983, for example, a Maputo businessman was arrested for smuggling offences. He apparently used a special refrigerated van to smuggle up to fifteen tonnes of prawns to Swaziland each week and, to ensure the smooth passage of his shellfish, he gave substantial bribes to customs and immigration officials. The businessman was tried in secret by a revolutionary tribunal and executed by firing squad. The execution alarmed the Asian business community and, presumably, fellow smugglers because the legislation which made the offence a capital one was passed retrospectively while the accused was in custody. Increasing shortages of foodstuffs and the spread of the black market prompted the government to take a firm stand and, to discourage others, the secret trial was followed by an execution broadcast on Maputo radio.

Public executions may or may not be consistent with the principles of Marxist-Leninism, but they perhaps suggest that corruption is neither encouraged nor condoned. But to test whether Afro-Marxist regimes can make serious or permanent reductions in the incidence of corruption requires a trial period of political and economic stability which the internal and external opponents of these regimes are unlikely to grant.

D. Corruption and Kleptocracy; the case of Nigeria

A Nigerian businessman recently appealed against his tax assessment on the grounds that he had a wife, two children, and three civil servants to support. The tax inspector allowed the appeal on the understanding that the businessman now had a wife, two children and four civil servants to support.

When foreign visitors to Nigeria have finished complaining about Lagos and its traffic jams, heat and humidity, power cuts and open drains, it is usually time for the travellers' tales of voracious and pervasive corruption. This is not to suggest that corruption is unimportant, but rather to emphasise that it is particularly conspicuous and well publicised in Nigeria. The controversy surrounding the attempted kidnapping of the Nigerian politician, Umaru Dikko, has only confirmed the popular impression that corruption in Nigeria is endemic and uncontrollable. It may be conceded that the level of corruption has varied over time, but the usual inference is that the variation is only between extremely high and unbelievably high.

As early as 1955, the Prime Minister of the Eastern Region of Nigeria appointed a judicial commission to inquire into allegations of corruption in all aspects of public life in the region. In 1961, the Eastern Nigerian Development Board loaned one million pounds to a private company, but omitted to mention this in its annual report because the Chairman of the company and the Board were one and the same person. In the interests of geographic balance, (always a sensitive matter in Nigeria), it should perhaps be noted that, in 1962, over two million pounds was diverted from the Western Nigerian Development Corporation into the accounts of a private company (West Africa, July 4th, 1970, p.729). (15) Thus, before independence and well before the oil boom, corruption was a conspicuous fact of Nigerian public life.

To explain why Nigeria has proved so susceptible to corruption requires a far reaching examination of Nigerian political history. (16) For present purposes, some central ingredients of such an explanation seem immediately available and it can safely be asserted that corruption in Nigeria has something to do with the divisive nature of colonial rule and the uneven development of the territories which eventually made up independent Nigeria. The political and administrative legacy of colonial rule was to structure political competition along regional and ethnic lines and to ensure that federalism, in the Nigerian context, would degenerate into a fight for spoils. Given Nigeria's area and population, it was inevitable that competitive elections would be expensive affairs and that the struggle to acquire campaign finance would almost necessarily involve the diversion of public funds. Where political conflict revolves around issues other than ideological or religious principle, it follows that, to attract and retain friends and followers, the politically ambitious require funds and resources. Obviously, the holders of public office do not have to look too far for a ready supply of patronage resources and other benefits.

But colonial rule and the consequent structure and nature of political competition provide only some of the necessary ingredients. The Nigerian economy displays more clearly, and on a grander scale, the many problems of underdevelopment. (17) The overwhelmingly commercial, rather than industrial, character of Nigerian capitalism makes the commission payment and the introduction fee major forms of economic endeavour. Outside of construction projects, to be a businessman is to be a trader, a dealer, a distributor or a middleman. When the main body of productive investment derives from the government, it necessarily attracts ambitious entrepreneurs anxious to ensure that contracts, licenses and allocations are directed to the most profitable channels. The development of Nigerian capitalism has been documented elsewhere, but it is worth noting that, even before the oil boom, Nigerian businessmen fed off the body politic and the discovery of oil simply ensured that the parasites grew fatter and more bloated.

The growth of capitalism had obvious consequences for the emergence of a large, urban elite who acquired strong vested interests in the maintenance of existing economic arrangements and policies. But it is worth observing that the corruption of the elite was facilitated, even encouraged, by popular attitudes toward the acquisition and ostentatious display of private wealth. As Dudley has observed, there is 'some ambivalence about corruption amongst Nigerians' (1982, p.28). In many cases, it seems that public attitudes are shaped more by the use made of wealth than by how it is acquired. Where a 'big man' flaunts his corruptly acquired wealth, but simultaneously distributes some benefits and favours to his family and community, he is unlikely to be condemned. Condemnation from 'outsiders' is likely to be interpreted as symptomatic of jealousy or envy rather than indicative of a disinterested devotion to the public interest. (18)

Political and economic factors have combined to produce an environment characterised by sharp inequalities between the urban centres and the countryside, by 'public squalor and private affluence' and by apparently chronic political instability. Nigeria has been afflicted by sporadic outbreaks of communal violence as well as by the slaughter of civil war and attempted secession. The corruption and regional and ethnic bias associated with the civilian politicians of the immediate post-independence years contributed to the increasing readiness of the military to intervene in dramatic fashion. Successive military regimes have proclaimed their disinterested concern for the interests of the nation and their detestation of the narrow, self-serving and factional squabbles of politicians.

If politics in Nigeria is frequently associated with corruption, patronage and the pursuit of spoils, the purportedly non-political military rulers of Nigeria have, with one brief exception, largely been tarred with the same brush. But it is also interesting to note that, while the military rulers have enjoyed no more success in reducing corruption than their civilian counterparts, it seems clear that Nigeria has been spared a ruling military predator of the stature of Mobutu in Zaire and Acheampong in Ghana. Corruption has flourished under civilian and military rulers alike, but it has not been organised or directed by a single individual or 'family' as it has been in some other African states. Nigeria is too large, too diverse, and too volatile to succumb easily to the embrace of a corrupt dictator, but then the same factors militate against the efforts of all its rulers whatever their intentions.

There seems little doubt that an unusual combination of historical, political, economic and social factors has produced a polity in which corruption seems almost inevitable. But the present and recent problems of Nigeria are the product of specific and unique developments and policies as well as the consequences of underlying structural and environmental conditions. If the oil boom did not instigate corruption in Nigeria, it certainly accelerated and expanded it. Almost overnight, it seemed that money was no object, that the normal financial constraints no longer applied. Federal revenues increased twenty-two fold

between 1967-77 and capital spending jumped from three billion
naira in 1970-75 to an estimated thirty billion naira in 1975-80
(Panter-Brick,(ed), 1978, p.1).

Oil money generated a consumer spending spree amongst the
urban elite and fortunes were rapidly acquired in property
speculation, building and contracting and in commerce. At the
same time, there was a collapse in both agricultural production
and exports and a sharp increase in food imports. Oil exports
reached 90% of total exports by 1974 and, by 1978, Lagos airport
was dealing almost exclusively with imported rather than exported
goods. While the oil money flowed, the sharp and growing
imbalance in the non-oil trade seemed a matter of small concern
to the political and commercial elite who were preoccupied by the
additional opportunities presented by the Indigenisation Decree of
1972. Not only were the procedures for share acquisition widely
abused through fraudulent applications in the names of servants or
even pets, but many Nigerians 'earned lucrative rewards for
cooperating in asset transfer arrangements to the foreign firms'
(Young, 1982, p. 229). Thus, as a group, Nigerian businessmen
were substantially enriched by a public policy ostensibly aimed at
curbing foreign ownership and restoring Nigerian assets to the
Nigerian 'people'. The consequences of the Indigenisation Decree
offered further proof of the applicability to Nigeria of the
'Matthew Principle', to them that hath it shall be given.

By the mid-1970s, the corruption associated with the Gowon
regime, if not with General Gowon himself, had reached amazing
proportions and events like the Cement Scandal discussed earlier
confirmed popular impressions that the riches of the oil economy
were being siphoned off by a parasitic elite at an alarming rate.
To one observer, the oil boom had the effect of converting 'the
military-political decision makers and their bureaucratic aides into
a new property owning, rentier class working in close and direct
collaboration with foreign business interests with the sole aim of
expropriating the surplus derived from oil for their private and
personal benefit' (Dudley, 1982, p.116). Corruption in contracting,
construction and in government purchasing and distribution became
pervasive and stories like the one at the beginning of this chapter
began to circulate. If corruption is a cancer, Nigeria was riddled
with it at the height of the oil boom.

But the overthrow of Gowon, the drastic surgery performed on
the public sector by his successor, Murtala Mohammed, the return
of civilian rule and the end of the oil boom did not prove enough
to make a serious impact on corruption in Nigeria. The elections
of 1979 and 1983 were both characterised by widespread corruption,
ballot-rigging and coercion and, when the Nigerian military seized
power again in 1983, it was not entirely unexpected. The main
justification offered for Nigeria's most recent military coup was

the allegedly rampant corruption associated with the Shagari regime of 1979-83. The early months of the new military government under General Buhari were devoted in part to the prosecution of a number of leading politicians and businessmen on charges of corruption and economic 'sabotage', but some leading political figures, like Umaru Dikko, managed to evade arrest and make their way abroad.

The charges against Umaru Dikko and others revealed how, even in days of relative austerity, public office or access to public office in Nigeria affords ample opportunities for large-scale corruption. One of the 'wanted' men, Isiyaku Ibrahim, a wealthy businessman and former executive committee member of the National Party of Nigeria (NPN), has revealed that he launched his business career by means of an unsolicited 'birthday gift' of a quarter of a million dollars from a French businessman (West Africa, 23rd January, 1984, p. 186). Umaru Dikko has explained the delivery of suitcases full of money to his home as no more than voluntary, legal campaign contributions. He further observed that, 'Just because money was delivered to my house boy doesn't mean it was for me' (quoted in West Africa, 25th February, 1985).

The main charges against Dikko involve what has become known as the 'Rice Scandal' (New African, April 1985, pp. 17-18) during his period as Chairman of the Presidential Task Force on Rice. Ironically, the ostensible point of setting up the task force was to find ways of stabilising the price of rice. In practice, the distribution of rice became a question of party patronage or simple bribery and the rice distributors passed on their extra 'costs' in terms of inflated prices. The sums involved seem considerable and one charge suggests that Dikko received over four million naira for one rice contract with a firm called Eurotrade Nigeria Ltd. This firm admitted in a Lagos Court to making other substantial payments to Dikko and to NPN headquarters (The Observer, 17 February, 1985, p.8). When a relatively small trading company admits to having paid almost ten million dollars in bribes or 'campaign contributions', it 'gives one an idea of the rate of profit in their business, and indeed of the rate of profit for the much bigger fish - the international commodity traders' (New African, April, 1985, p.18).

It seems clear that the return to civilian rule in 1979 stimulated a renewed growth of corruption in Nigeria. Certain scandals such as the oil frauds discussed in an earlier chapter caused simmering discontent, but perhaps the most controversial episode concerned the 300 million pounds contract to buy Jaguar aircraft which involved an alleged 'commission' payment of no less than 22 million pounds. Some reports even suggest that the Jaguar Scandal actually precipitated the 1983 coup (West Africa, 26th March 1984, p. 691). Where corruption is endemic, stories about corruption abound and the scale of fraud and deception is often exaggerated in the re-telling. The efforts of the new regime to combat corruption will be evaluated in the next chapter, but it should be clear that Nigeria has endured unusually high levels of corruption for an unusually long period.

The easy money days of the oil boom have gone and oil exports, for example, have declined from $23 billion in 1980 to only $10 billion in 1983. It is now anticipated that almost half of Nigeria's oil revenues will be devoted to servicing the international debts which accrued during the boom years of the 1970s. It remains to be seen whether the regime can transform Nigeria's economic situation so as to satisfy the international finance institutions, the acquisitive urges of Nigeria's urban elite and the long neglected aspirations of the majority of the population. Such a balancing or reconciling of different interests may well prove an impossible task, but then the fight against corruption in Nigeria seems equally arduous.

E. Conclusion

The standard test for colour blindness requires individuals to determine whether a superficially random array of coloured spots conceals the outline of a number or letter. The ability to detect the patterns of different coloured spots which make up the number or letter is proof that the individual is free from this particular eye defect. But success in passing this test does not guarantee immunity from myopia, astigmatism or cataracts. In short, perfect vision requires more than the ability to identify patterns of spots.

The task of identifying patterns of political corruption presents a superficially similar problem in that the picture is initially confusing and bewildering. But the major difference is, of course, that the optician knows that patterns of spots exist on the cards before the tests are administered. In the case of corruption, it seems that the existence of such patterns is an unproven assumption. Thus, patterns of corruption often lie in the eye of the beholder. The Marxist leader or scholar 'knows' that corruption is not culturally determined and is certain that it represents a major mechanism for the accumulation of capital in dependent capitalist societies. But not all scholars accept the utility of such categories and the anthropologically inclined may see patterns of corrupt behaviour emanating from gift-giving and other expressions of loyalty (Ekpo (ed), 1979, pp. 161-188). Liberal economists identify the form and growth of corruption as a reaction to the regulatory activities of the African state and as indicative of the inexorable power of market forces. In short, students of corruption in Africa frequently find what they expect to find.

The brief sketches of politics and corruption in Kenya, Zambia, Nigeria and the Afro-Marxist states may be useful insofar as they suggest points of similarity and difference, but they are certainly not adequate substitutes for careful and thorough case studies of individual countries. If the analyst focuses on the points of similarity, it is possible to develop models, concepts or theories about corruption in Africa. But, if the differences are accentuated, then the picture blurs and we no longer see patterns but only spots. There are many different kinds of political regime in Africa and, as Crawford Young has convincingly demonstrated, these differences produce a wide variation of policy outcomes. Similarly, corruption varies in form, location, scale and impact. Indeed, it would seem inherently improbable for major differences in ideology, area and population, party structure, security and stability, customs and conventions, economic constraints and opportunities and political leadership not to have a considerable bearing on patterns of corruption in Africa.

It is clear, however, that in some countries certain themes predominate. There are obvious similarities between the official encouragement given to the entrepreneurial ambitions of politicians and officials in Kenya and Zambia and the seemingly pervasive capitalist ethos of Nigeria. Formal responses may vary, but there seem to be some grounds for believing that many African governments actively promote the development of an indigenous business class. In an underdeveloped economy, the centrality of the state in economic terms means that the seed capital for entrepreneurial endeavour must come from the public sector. Different countries pursue different methods, but among the most favoured are inflated and overpaid bureaucracies, privileged access to credit and subsidies, the transfer of foreign assets into selected local hands and a general indifference to the use of public funds and resources for private purposes. But it would be an exaggeration or even a mistake to claim that such practices form a general pattern of behaviour in Africa. Not only do 'capitalists' like Hastings Banda in Malawi enforce strict codes of conduct on public officials, but some of the Afro-Marxist states have made strenuous efforts to impede rather than encourage the emergence of an indigenous bourgeois class.

Marxist leaders tend to attribute corruption to capitalism and colonialism and to associated patterns of dependency and underdevelopment. Non-Marxist leaders usually see the problem in terms of individual morality rather than as systemic or structural. The best example is the Zambian leader, Kenneth Kaunda, who has elaborated his own ideology of 'humanism' which he sees more as 'an ethical stance, a mode of personal behaviour, than as a guideline for reorganising society' (Ottoway, 1981, p.44). Kaunda seems to believe that self-discipline and personal integrity are the keys to creating a new society in Zambia, but he largely ignores or rejects the view that structural and institutional reform may be necessary to allow or encourage the 'good' Zambian to emerge and flourish. If Kaunda's perspective on corruption is shared by other African leaders, it is hopefully an advance on General Mobutu's advice to Zairean civil servants that, 'If you want to steal, steal a little cleverly, in a nice way' (quoted in Gould, 1980, p. xiii).

While some African leaders are notoriously personally corrupt, it does not seem to follow that personal incorruptability, whether inspired by Marxist discipline or Christian morality, is a crucial factor in reducing the level of corruption. Corruption in Nigeria reached one of its cyclical peaks under the leadership of General Gowon, but it has not, to my knowledge, been argued that Gowon was personally corrupt. President Kaunda is known for his personal integrity but, like Gowon, he is often accused of condoning or failing to deter his corrupt associates. Similarly, Julius Nyerere in Tanzania and successive leaders in Angola and Mozambique have displayed high personal standards, but have enjoyed less than complete success in inculcating such standards into their governments and parties.

Political leadership in Africa is a notoriously precarious activity and it seems that, to maintain or consolidate their positions, many leaders who are not personally corrupt are obliged to distribute patronage and favours to reward followers, co-opt opponents, divert rivals and appease warring factions. The line between patronage and corruption is often blurred and easily crossed and both represent a rejection or departure from the Weberian ideal type of bureaucratic organisation. In unstable and dangerous political environments, the outstanding qualifications for preferment may be personal loyalty and, where a leader can rely on such loyalty, he may be willing to turn a blind eye to a variety of deficiencies, including the misuse of public office.

Where inter-party rather than intra-party contests for public office occur, it seems that high levels of electoral corruption are often found, not least because, in underdeveloped societies, there are few legitimate methods of filling campaign treasure chests. When the governing party receives the lion's share of 'donations', as in the case of Nigeria in 1983, and it has more money than it knows what to do with, then the surplus is likely to find its way into numbered private bank accounts. In Nigeria and Kenya, parties have tended to coalesce around ethnic and regional rather than ideological or class bases. National political conflict then takes the form of regional or ethnic rivalry and jealousy in the struggle to control the resources of the state. As a consequence, allegations of corruption can be more easily dismissed as being motivated by a desire to discredit the currently ruling regime or group. The patron-client relationships which helped cement the ruling party in Kenya after independence served to reinforce the perception that what was good for Kenyatta and his entourage was good for all Kikuyu.

In the one party states, the obvious tendency has been for party organisations to atrophy as instruments of mass mobilisation and become vehicles for individual advancement. In Kenya, Zambia and elsewhere, party membership is the necessary, if not sufficient, condition for achieving privileged access to education, employment, loans, licenses and contracts. In Marxist states, party membership itself is a privilege and ensures that party members will be treated differently.   Many African parties are no more than mechanisms for distributing patronage and leaders and followers are only held together by an uneasy mutual dependence.   But if the Africanisation of colonial bureaucracies and the indigenisation of foreign or non-citizen owned businesses has helped lubricate the machinery of clientelism, worsening economic crises make new demands more and more difficult to meet. The gross indebtedness of many African states is, in part, a consequence of their determination to borrow heavily abroad in order to maintain the incomes and life styles of their privileged groups. Where governments attempt a radical transformation of the status quo, they typically risk economic dislocation, military intervention, destabilisation and even civil war.   When staying afloat requires great skill and luck, piloting the ship of state to a new world through unchartered waters demands a clarity of vision, a steadfastness of purpose and a degree of external support that few African leaders have been able to acquire or display.

If different regimes pursue different policy choices, the outcomes of such policies have differing impacts on the patterns and incidence of corruption.   There seems little doubt that the development path chosen by Nigeria's military rulers during the oil boom years did much to aggravate the already significant problem of corruption.   But, as we have seen, there are no easy choices and different routes present their own costs and difficulties. There is, for example, some evidence to suggest that states which have chosen the 'capitalist' path, like Kenya, Nigeria and the Ivory Coast, have enjoyed higher growth rates than the 'socialist' states. But it also seems that the 'capitalist' states display grosser inequalities of income and higher levels of corruption.

The basic lesson of the four sketches seems to be that, despite some obvious points of similarity, there is no one pattern of corruption to be found in Africa, but rather a variety of patterns produced by political choices and differing pressures, constraints and opportunities.

NOTES

(1)   This is not to deny that Nkrumah was involved in a variety of corrupt transactions, (Le Vine, 1975, pp 28-29, 133-136), but merely to suggest that, in financial terms, his misdemeanours almost pale into insignificance when compared to the activities of some of his successors.

(2)   Self-definition poses certain problems, but the labels do not seem overly controversial when applied to Mozambique and Angola.

(3)   If Hoover's 'information' allowed him wide discretion in his direction of the Federal Bureau of Investigation, it did not seem to encourage any presidential ambitions.

(4)   The debate about the character of the 'Mau Mau' continues, but (Rosberg and Nottingham, 1966; Barnett and Njama, 1966) make useful starting points.

(5)   The land issue is extensively discussed, from contrasting perspectives, in (Harbeson, 1973; and Wasserman 1976).

(6)   The purpose of the land transfers was, in part, 'to provide an idigenous breakwater against future waves of mass agitation' (Wasserman, 1976, p. 173).

(7)   This belated realisation did not, of course, prevent the earlier imprisonment of Kaunda and Harry Nkumbula. The road to independence is described in (Mulford, 1967).

(8)   The point here is to contrast the Zambian experience with that of the Portugese colonies and is not intended to suggest that the anti-colonial struggle was the exclusive preserve of a politically conscious nationalist elite. For evidence of the attitudes and actions of rural villagers, see (Rasmussen in Tordoff (ed), 1974, pp. 40-61).

(9)   The creation of the one-party state helped to avert the danger of the fragmentation of UNIP, but it did not, of course, eliminate political opposition. One important consequence was to change the balance of power between party officials and civil servants in the latter's favour and, therefore, the former's access to patronage and other state resources was correspondingly reduced. These developments are perceptively discussed in (Scott in Tordoff (ed), 1980, pp. 139-161).

(10)   The problems of the parastatal sector in Zambia are outlined in (Johns in Tordoff (ed), 1980, pp.104-129).

(11)   The severe economic crises of recent years have ensured
         that the pool of patronage has steadily evaporated. One
         consequence is to intensify factional competition in
         pursuit of diminishing resources.

(12)   The limitations, biases and omissions of much of the
         recent literature on southern Africa is convincingly
         exposed in (White, 1985, pp. 320-332).

(13)   Ideological supporters of such governments tend to use
         capitalism and colonialism as explanations of all manner
         of social evils including alcoholism and prostitution.
         Recent examples are (Isaacman and Isaacman, 1983, p.
         58-59).

(14)   One study has concluded that 'the campaign against
         corruption and the betrayal of the public trust is a
         central and highly visible theme in Mozambique's political
         life. Moreover, the highest levels of the government
         have been remarkably free from both corruption and
         intrigue' (Isaacman and Isaacman, 1983, p. 143).

(15)   The issues of communalism and regionalism in Nigeria are
         explored in (Melson and Wolpe (eds), 1971). The
         contributions by (Sklar, pp 514-529; and O'Connell, pp.
         629-672) are particularly useful.

(16)   An indispensable guide to pre-independence Nigerian
         political history is (Coleman, 1958). A recent general
         history from an African perspective is (Isichei, 1983).

(17)   This is a large subject but the penetrating and provocative
         analysis in (Williams, 1976) merits careful attention.

(18)   Not only are corrupt officials sometimes admired for their
         entrepreneurial flair but communal norms make it 'fairly
         easy for corrupt officials to gain sympathy and support by
         sharing their gains with relatives and making donations to
         home-town improvements' (Peil, 1976, p. 56).

(19)   The economic policies and processes of this period are
         discussed in (Panter-Brick (ed), 1978), and the chapter by
         (Turner, pp. 166-197) is particularly illuminating about the
         mechanics of corruption .

6 Controlling corruption: prophylactics and panaceas

Nearly all African political leaders, except perhaps the notorious President Mobutu of Zaire, publicly condemn corruption. In some cases, the condemnation seems ritualistic and rhetorical and is not accompanied by any change in economic or political institutions and practices. But it has to be recognised that, for example, President Nyerere has taken steps in an effort to arrest and retard the tide of corruption which has engulfed some of Tanzania's neighbours. (1) The results of governmental drives against corruption in Africa have, to say the least, been disappointing and, where the levels of corruption have apparently been temporarily reduced, the reduction has arguably been achieved at an unacceptably high political, economic and administrative cost. The initial purpose of this chapter is to examine the different strategies governments have employed against corruption and to evaluate their utility. The final section of the chapter will consider the place of corruption in African politics and explore the conditions which sustain and nurture it.

But, at the outset, it may be useful to offer a cautionary reminder and emphasise that the task of identifying levels of corruption and even determining whether particular events or transactions involve corrupt inducements is fraught with difficulty. By its nature, corruption resists easy or precise measurement and identification. Things are not always as they appear and, in regard to the incidence of corruption, there is often smoke without fire. More literally, fire itself is sometimes a smokescreen and the evidence to prove alleged corruption is destroyed. After the 1983 coup in Nigeria, for example, Major-General Buhari and the evidence to prove alleged corruption is destroyed. After the 1983 coup in Nigeria, for example, Major-General Buhari asserted that the fires which had gutted the Federal Ministry of Education, the Nigerian External Telecommunications building and the Federal Capital Development Authority's accounts office were proof that 'Arson has been used to cover up fraudulent acts in public institutions' (quoted in West Africa, January 9th, 1984, p. 57).

Events which have every appearance of being conspicuous examples of large-scale corruption may, on closer examination, be attributable to other causes. In 1980, the apparent 'disappearance' of almost three billion naira from the accounts of the Nigerian National Petroleum Corporation (NNPC) produced such a chorus of allegations and condemnations in the Nigerian press that, with the memories of the 1975 Cement Racket fresh in the public's mind, the government was forced to appoint a high-level judicial commission to investigate. To the government's relief and many people's surprise, the Irikefe Commission found no evidence of corruption and dismissed the allegations as 'the greatest hoax of all time' (quoted in West Africa, August 18th, 1980, p. 1535). But while doubts have subsequently been raised about the veracity of this particular finding, the other conclusions of the inquiry have not been challenged. The Irikefe Commission found that the NNPC had no proper accounting system, and a severe shortage of professionally qualified staff. In short, the accounts department of the organisation responsible for the bulk of government revenue was in complete disarray. In such circumstances, opportunities for corruption are plentiful while the means of identifying its occurrence and detecting the perpetrators are hopelessly inadequate.

Although Nigeria often provides conspicuous examples, the problem of identifying fraud and misuse of public funds is a general one. If the spate of fires in Nigerian public buildings suggests attempts to destroy incriminating evidence, there is, in many other instances, simply no evidence to destroy. Few African states possess bureaucracies motivated and equipped to produce regular audited accounts and, more commonly, the accounts of government departments and especially parastatals are so long delayed that the transactions they purport to describe have become of purely historical interest. In the absence of accurate and up-to-date financial information, allegations of corruption from persons who are rarely disinterested are hard to evaluate. Capital accumulation takes a variety of forms in Africa and, if corruption is a method of acquiring financial capital, allegations of corruption are not infrequently attempts to make political capital. (2)

If reliable information is hard to acquire, a popular governmental response is to establish commissions of inquiry. Such commissions have proved a major growth industry, especially in West Africa, and their reports usually receive wide publicity. For the most part, such commissions are concerned to name the 'guilty' men and to document their crimes but, occasionally, they venture more general conclusions about the social and political significance of pervasive corruption. Corruption inquiries, it should be noted, always concern other people. Corrupt political leaders almost never instigate inquiries into their own affairs unless they are certain to produce a cosmetic exoneration. In the case of Sierra Leone, it has been argued that commissions of inquiry are appointed when one of three conditions applies: 'firstly, when a "scandal" becomes public ...; secondly, when a change of government takes place and political advantage can be gained and thirdly, when serious financial loss or inefficiency is known about by senior figures (and to a certain extent a process of face-saving has to take place) (Riley in Clarke (ed), 1983, pp. 195-196). Riley's conditions seem to be of more general applicability and confirm that merely appointing a judge to conduct an inquiry does not prove that the exercise is somehow neutral or non-political. The creation, structure and scope of commissions of inquiry are the products of political choices based, for the most part, on partisan considerations.

Commissions of inquiry do not then present comprehensive, balanced or fair assessments of the incidence of corruption. Where corruption pervades the highest levels of any African regime, inquiries are anathema. But when regimes have been overthrown by force, the coup-makers frequently instigate inquiries into the activities of the overthrown regime to discredit its leaders and legitimate military intervention. In most cases, inquiries focus on the activities of wicked, greedy or sinful individuals, rather than on structural or systemic considerations, because the normal operating assumption is that the behaviour is deviant rather than standard practice. When disposing of the 'rotten apples', the soundness of the barrel is rarely questioned. Where the concept of the commission of inquiry is overused, it loses what shreds of credibility it once possessed and when, as in Nigeria, 'a commission completed its inquiries into 74 organisations in only 6 months' (New African Development, June 1977, p. 529), the exercise verges on the farcical.

The response of new political leaders to the corruption of their predecessors can, on occasion, be abrupt and severe as, for example, when Flight Lieutenant Jerry Rawlings executed three former heads of state in Ghana. (3) But if Rawlings' ruthless and dramatic response excited international attention and comment, other African leaders have sought to purge the allegedly corrupt members of their governments and bureaucracies by less extreme means. When General Gowon's regime in Nigeria was overthrown in 1975, the new leader, Murtala Mohammed, embarked upon

'Operation Purge the Nation' which aimed at removing the corrupt and incompetent from the civil service, the statutory corporations, the customs service and a variety of other public institutions. An estimated 11,000 persons were dismissed from their posts and over half the heads of the civil service departments were 'retired' or dismissed. Mohammed's actions were an understandable and popular response to the prevailing complaint that 'Corruption, indiscipline and needless arrogance not only abound in the Nigerian civil service; it has become an abode for mediocrity, laziness, apathy, avoidable narrow-mindedness, nepotism, favouritism and tribalism on a stupendous and incredible scale' (Sunday Times, (Nigeria), November 9, 1975).

If the immediate impact of 'Operation Purge the Nation' was that 'for the first time civil servants went to work on time, politely attended to their duties and everything started to move' (Olowu, 1983, p. 294), there is no convincing evidence to suggest that it had an enduring or substantial effect on the level of corruption. In fact, the purge was less radical than first publicised both because many civil servants left with full retirement benefits and because the dismissals were followed by a relatively small number of prosecutions. When civil servants are liable to dismissal on the basis of unsubstantiated allegations, it provides numerous opportunities to settle personal grudges and encourages unjustified victimisation. In practice, the purge may well have been counter-productive in that it dislocated the functioning of the bureaucracy and required the possibly over-rapid promotion of junior officials to senior positions. (4)

It came as no particular suprise when, in 1975, the new military leaders emphasised the role of discipline in improving efficiency and reducing corruption. But when the leader of the 1983 coup waged his own 'War Against Indiscipline' (WAI), it did not command any sustained popular enthusiasm. WAI was led by Major-General Idiagbon and concentrated on economic sabotage, ostentatious living, petty corruption and disorderliness such as queue jumping at bus stops. The emphasis of WAI on what appeared to be trivialities caused many to ridicule the campaign and ask "Why WAI?' or to rename it 'War Against Idiagbon'. (5)

The Buhari regime, which came to power at the end of 1983, did more than launch the 'War Against Indiscipline', it arrested, detained and tried a large number of politicians and businessmen on charges of 'economic crimes' before special military tribunals. The tribunals have sentenced a number of former state governors to long terms of imprisonment for extorting political contributions from contractors but, while former President Shagari has been detained, no charges have as yet been preferred against him or Vice-President Dr. Ekwume. The tribunals have certainly punished a number of 'guilty men', but it is hard to escape observing that the corruption trials have concentrated on governors of the southern based opposition parties. Some commentators have noted an affinity between the northern domination of the present military government and the northern dominated National Party of Nigeria (NPN) led by former President Shagari. It has even been alleged that southern political leaders instigated the attempted kidnapping of Umaru Dikko because, 'If Dikko were to be repatriated, charges against other northern leaders, including Shagari, could not be avoided (New Statesman, 22nd February, 1985, p. 20). Thus, what is presented by the 'non-political' military government as a disinterested search for 'guilty men' is seen by the regime's opponents as a selective, partisan method of punishing political rivals while, at the same time, protecting regional allies.

If Nigerian military leaders have laboured the virtues of discipline and circumvented legal procedures to imprison allegedly corrupt politicians, their response at least signifies a willingness to act. The problem with the preceding civilian regime was that its response to corruption was characterised by 'structural formalism' (Aina, 1982, p. 74). The regime passed laws and issued orders and decrees directed at reducing corruption, but there was no serious attempt to ensure that such provisions were implemented. The extent of the neglect can be measured by the fact that between 1979 and 1983 only the President and Vice-President declared their assets when the 1979 constitution prescribed that all public servants declare their assets within six months. As an editorial in West Africa observed, 'the non-functioning of the Code of Conduct Bureau with its empty vaults awaiting declarations of assets that were never made proved to be a symbol of the good intentions of the 1979 constitution and the inability to deliver of the ensuing regime' (9th January, 1984).

But, in discussing political responses to corruption, it is precisely the nature of 'the inability to deliver' that is at issue. Political leaders may claim to have done their utmost to stamp out corruption, but blame indiscipline or immorality for their failure. In practice, 'structural formalism' is characteristic of many regimes in Africa and, where corruption becomes a matter of widespread public concern, governments may wish to be seen to be dealing with it. This desire may be present both when the government has no faith in the methods it prescribes and when self-interest precludes effective action.

A favoured device of a variety of regimes is some kind of leadership code which places certain restrictions on the activities of government ministers and senior officials. Such codes also often require politicians and civil servants to register their business interests and property holdings. In Tanzania, the code precludes political leaders and bureaucrats from owning more than one home, from being directors of private businesses, from owning shares and from receiving more than one salary. While there is no doubt that President Nyerere has fully supported the idea of a leadership code, he found it necessary to impose it on his party's executive committee and to override the opposition of some members of his Cabinet. If the political leader's perception of the importance of such codes is not fully supported by his closest associates and lieutenants, the task of implementing the provisions of the code is likely to prove insuperable. Leadership codes are rarely comprehensive and, even where they appear so, they tend not be be implemented in full. They can nearly always be circumvented and, even in Tanzania, it seems that property and business interests are readily transferred into the names of relatives and friends. In Zambia, as we have seen, the leadership code contains no procedure for its enforcement and there have therefore never been any prosecutions under its provisions. Leadership codes are another aspect of 'structural formalism' and the consequence is that they are honoured more in the breach than the observance.

It may well be the case that purges and deterrent sentencing have a short-term impact on the level of corruption but, by themselves, it seems unlikely that, in the longer run, they do more than introduce a note of caution and decorum into corrupt transactions. They neither address the problem of detection nor change the range of pressures, incentives and opportunities which encourage corruption. Those who engage in criminal pursuits do not do so in the expectation they will be caught, let alone punished. In most cases, the origins of corruption seem to be too firmly embedded in the body politic to be extracted by anything less than major political and economic surgery. While the basic conditions and structures of African societies remain unaltered, the 'short, sharp, shocks' favoured by so many African regimes will have about as much impact on corruption as capital punishment did on the incidence of sheep stealing in eighteenth century England. In medical terms, while the symptoms of corruption can occasionally be distressing or embarrassing for Africa's ruling elites, they still prefer to risk a possibly terminal military 'stroke' rather than undergo surgery which would threaten their material as opposed to physical well-being. In short, when the structures and policies of a state are designed to serve the interests of particular groups, reform proposals which endanger those interests do not appear on the political agenda.

Commissions of inquiry charged with investigating corruption rarely offer much in the way of general explanations of its 'causes'. When they do, it is not surprising that, given their political origins, the findings of such inquiries are often expressed in terms of general cultural and social characteristics rather than the identification of particular groups, policies or structures. One of Ghana's major inquiries concluded, for instance, that 'the prevalence of bribery and corruption in contemporary Ghanaian society ... is attributable, less to the content or defect of our existing laws and procedures, but more to our ingrained social habits; attitudes of accommodation and compromise; our misguided sympathy for wrong-doers and reluctance to expose them; our greed, and sheer materialism; our lust for wealth and power ...' (quoted in West Africa, 1st December, 1975, pp. 1430-1431). Blaming values and attitudes or habits and customs spreads rather than focuses responsibility for corruption.   If society is to blame, then changes in policy or personnel are bound to be superficial and superfluous.

The implication of the above perspective seems to be that, without some radical moral re-armament, the problem of corruption will continue to grow. But the inequalities, uncertainties and shortages which afflict so many African states suggest that any new moral order will take a very long time to emerge.   Where corruption offers the possibility of economic salvation or even survival, it seems at least optimistic to imagine that 'ingrained social habits' will change without some major alterations to the environment which generates and sustains such habits.

If corrupt or myopic political leaders recommend inadequate and misconceived strategies for tackling corruption, academic analysts display a similar enthusiasm for unrealistic remedies. One recent account suggests that 'corruption will be most prevalent when salaries are low, opportunities great, and policing weak; it will be infrequent when the reverse applies, and salaries are generous, opportunities few, and policing strong' (Palmier in Clarke (ed), 1983, p. 209). While there may be some analytical merit in such categories, it is difficult to see their relevance when applied to the realities of modern Africa. When levels of corruption are high, how can policing be anything other than weak? If salaries are already high, as they are in Africa, how much higher do they have to be to inhibit officials from accepting corrupt inducements? Palmier argues that 'A generous salary may not only reduce the attraction of opportunities: fear of its loss may act as a powerful element in policing' (1983, p. 209), but it may equally be argued that high salaries encourage corrupt competition for posts, facilitate business connections with potential corruptors in the private sector, and enable officials to purchase immunity from prosecution.

Students of bureaucratic corruption tend to treat 'politics' either as an additional, external factor to be weighed in the balance or as some kind of infection which erodes administrative efficiency and integrity. The essay by Palmier, for example, not only maintains a somewhat outmoded distinction between politics and administration, but his line of argument appears to suggest that the politicisation of bureaucracy, if not actually a crime in itself, is the major problem. If this is a reasonable interpretation, it would seem to follow that, to reduce corruption, we need to keep politics out of government. But because so many opportunities for corruption are presented by the expansion of public ownership and regulation, it seems that we need not only to keep politics out of government, but to keep the government out of the economy. In an ideal world, such advice would perhaps have a place but, in modern Africa, the prospects for either reform are so remote as to make their discussion an indulgence. Bureaucracy remains not merely an instrument for the formulation and execution of government policy, but an important arena for political competition and the major avenue for individual enrichment in Africa.

Academic specialisation tends both to narrow the focus and exaggerate the claims made on behalf of different disciplines. While students of public administration place great store by reforms in administrative structure, process, recruitment and remuneration, economists are likely to disparage such institutional tinkering. Obviously, where there are disputes about the origins and character of corruption in Africa, there will be conflicts over treatment. If, as we saw earlier, corruption is understood as a product of immorality and bad habits, the prescribed remedy may take the form of uplifting moral and ethical instruction for both officials and the public. But the numerous courses in administrative ethics offered at African institutes of public administration since independence do not seem to have achieved the desired effect. It is possible that the courses themselves are insufficiently intensive or rigorous, but it seems plausible to suggest that human weakness and greed is more likely to be a necessary rather than a sufficient condition for corruption.

Conversely, to identify the likely conditions under which corruption can be controlled is to demonstrate how far most African states are from achieving them. The control of corruption seems to require a combination of factors to operate simultaneously and amongst them are 'a population sufficiently alert, self-confident and politically aware to ... "blow the whistle", and determined enough to require effective redress. At the same time the state must be sufficiently open to allow such protests and to act effectively upon them' (Clarke (ed), 1983, p. xvi). No African state possesses such characteristics or enjoys the kind of relationship between governors and governed defined by such conditions.

If contemporary African conditions appear to militate against the effective control of corruption, there are always those who take the more comforting and reassuring long view. If corruption is perceived as a phase characteristic of 'development' or 'modernisation' which the developed states have already passed through, it is presumed by 'forward-looking' observers that Africa will enjoy a similar passage to virtue. Leaving aside the distinctly contentious notion that, for example, the United States has passed through its corrupt 'phase', the projections about Africa seem to be based on a set of optimistic and unlikely propositions. One recent study confidently asserts that 'There is reason to expect that good government in Nigeria will slowly replace the widespread corruption ... because (it is) the product of a materialism and a political fragmentation which will pass in development' (Brownsberger, 1983, p. 221). As Brownsberger sees it, time is the key to controlling corruption because, as time passes, all sorts of wonderful things are likely to happen, for example, 'As development progresses, the elite will grow broader, and so less alienated and less driven to ostentation' (p.231). Better still, 'nepotistic and party building corruption will diminish as opportunities outside the state expand' (p.231) The net result of this happy combination of circumstances is that 'Nigerians will enter government who have already fulfilled their material ambitions. They will identify not with an alienated elite of bureaucrats, but with the process by which they built their lives; they may be conservative but not corrupt' (p.232). This may all come to pass but, unfortunately for Nigeria, Brownsberger has even less control over the future than successive Nigerian regimes have had over corruption. Recent events in Nigeria indeed suggest that 'party building corruption will diminish,' not as Brownsberger argues, because 'development' makes it less necessary, but because military rule prohibits party formation.

While it is possible to resist Brownsberger's Reagan-tinted vision of Africa's future, it should be recognised both that the view enjoys influential support in the international finance institutions and that the central thesis merits serious consideration. If, as we have seen, rigorous statutes, wholesale purges, leadership codes and anti-corruption agencies have enjoyed little enduring impact on levels of corruption in Africa, it seems more probable, as Brownsberger suggests, that corruption will decline as a consequence of major political and economic change rather than in response to specific anti-corruption measures. Where corruption is the rule rather than the exception, attempts to treat it in isolation are unlikely to prove successful.

The real debate therefore concerns not the utility of different anti-corruption measures, but the kinds of systemic, structural and policy changes likely to produce substantial improvements in economic conditions and political relationships. In such a debate, corruption is reduced to a side issue and the arguments focus on how best to eliminate poverty, reduce inequality and lessen dependence. In short, the level of corruption is seen as a symptom of underdevelopment and its reduction is related to evaluations of the competing paths to 'development'.

In crude terms, there are one and a half views on how such goals can be accomplished. One is the 'capitalist' view sketched by Brownsberger above, while the other is the 'socialist' or 'left' view. Perhaps unfairly, the latter is characterised as only half a view because it seems to be undergoing a radical reappraisal. The problems and disappointments associated in the 1960s and 1970s with Nkrumah's Ghana, Nyerere's Tanzania and, more recently, with Machel's Mozambique have caused a number of 'socialist' analysts to revise their views. Many are as disenchanted with the performance of the state sector and as appalled at the depredations of the 'bureaucratic bourgeoisie' as their 'capitalist' colleagues. (6)   In 'left' circles, the call is for a 'genuine' or 'authentic' socialist transformation in Africa rather than ritual support of the centralisation of political and economic power in what are increasingly seen as parasitic hands. But the problems are considerable and, if 'massive state power, a coherent revolutionary ideology and effective leadership are the crucial organisational elements that foster the success of attempts at socialist transformation' (Callaghy in Rosberg and Callaghy (eds), 1979, p. 118), few African states can hope to succeed.   In circumstances, the leading Afro-Marxist regimes seem in need of considerable external support to survive, let alone effect comprehensive transformations of their societies.

The 'capitalist' view suggests, as a general principle, that government in Africa undertakes tasks it is poorly equipped to perform. It not only attempts too much, but what it does do, it normally does badly. The lesson which is often drawn is that, in the economic sphere, many tasks should be left to the disciplines and incentives of the market because 'By shifting some activities to private hands, significant gains in output may be possible with relatively little sacrifice of sociopolitical objectives' (World Bank, 1981, p. 37).   The assertion is that reliance on the private sector will produce significantly faster development and one consequence will be to reduce the attractions of the public sector as a source of status, wealth and power. A decline in corruption will be a by-product of the success of private enterprise in overcoming Africa's economic problems.   The faster growth rate of, for example, Kenya compared to Tanzania may strengthen the capitalist case but, if corruption is supposed to decline as development proceeds, Kenya clearly has some considerable way to go.

There are obvious objections to any simple association of levels of corruption with degrees and rates of development. Not only is the notion of development notoriously problematical, but economic comparisons reveal no clear patterns or correlations. If corruption is in some way a symptom of underdevelopment, it is not true to say that the poorest states have the highest levels of corruption. If it is reasonable to concede that rapid economic growth of the kind generated by abundant oil revenues multiplies opportunities for corruption, recession and stagnation do not appear to have much effect in discouraging it. Economic crises may threaten the survival of regimes, but they do not seem to impinge directly on the incidence of corruption. (7)

In practice, 'development' continues to elude all types of political regime and therefore its impact on levels of corruption in Africa remains to be proved. Not only do all African regimes, whatever their ostensible ideological plumage, possess large state sectors, but equally none has been able to eradicate capitalistic attitudes and tendencies. The effective choice seems to be less which road to development to take as how to make continuing underdevelopment marginally more comfortable. But political leaders still make choices and it may be useful to inquire, within the obvious structural and environmental constraints, why leaders make the choices they do. Why, in particular, do they seem unable or unwilling to embark on processes of political and economic change likely to reduce levels of corruption?

There are, of course, a number of possible answers to such deceptively simple questions and, while some focus on different aspects of what increasingly appears to be a common predicament, other answers are mutually incompatible. Simplistically, the reason why political leaders fail to choose any one set of policies is because they have chosen another set. But this not only begs the question of why one set and not another, it implies both that conscious judgement is being exercised and that those responsible possess some degree of discretion and authority in making such decisions.

Put differently, political leaders may make certain decisions either because they feel compelled to by external or internal coercion and pressure or because they prefer one set of policy goals to another. The status of corruption clearly varies in such calculations from being a trivial irrelevance not to be weighed in assessing competing strategies to, in the extreme case like Zaire, almost the raison d'etre of the regime. The implications in terms of policy focus also vary, from the corrupt regime which seeks solely to channel corruption, to the 'honest' reforming regime like that of Jerry Rawlings in Ghana which seek to curb corruption while simultaneously attempting to revitalise a moribund economy.

If curbing corruption is never more than one political objective among many, it is often less. If the failure of a variety of regimes to control corruption is conspicuous, it is only one failure among many. To know what needs to be done is not the same as being able to do it. Thus prescriptions for fighting corruption and blueprints for development are frequently insensitive to the very limited capacity of many African states to implement effectively any policy. Just because 'the term "bureaucratic state" describes both the form and the location of power in the African polity' (Crook in Lyon and Manor (eds), 1983, p. 186) does not mean that African bureaucracies possess more than very limited penetrative and coercive capabilities. If African states are authoritarian, they frequently lack authority.

The problem is twofold; first, political leaders have difficulty in ensuring that their subordinates carry out designated tasks; second, even where compliance is forthcoming, the bureaucratic apparatus lacks the resources, information and expertise to translate political aspirations into administrative reality. Thus, the coercive and repressive image of many regimes disguises their underlying impotence. When the mask of rhetoric slips, we learn, for example, that 'It was the weakness of the Nkrumah regime in its inability to control what went on rather than its totalitarian facade which facilitated corruption' (Werlin, 1972, p. 261). In the bureaucratic state, the role of potential rivals, like opposition parties and trade unions, is diminished and they are too feeble to compel the bureaucracy to meet any external standards. Without external controls and independent centres of power, 'bureaucratic factions blossom luxuriantly and each division of the apparatus becomes a virtual feudal domain that may parasitically exploit its clientele or the portion of the economy over which it wields power' (Scott, 1972, p.15)

Although government often assumes a bureaucratic form in Africa, it rarely behaves in accordance with the principles and procedures of Weber's ideal type. Formal rules frequently have little impact on the conduct of politicians and bureaucrats and, where lip service is paid to constitutional rule, the constitutions either allow great discretion to the political leader or otherwise prove adaptable to specific political needs. In practice, governments and their bureaucracies are held together, less by any shared commitment to sets of impersonal rules or codes of ethics, as by personalistic and particularistic considerations.

The connections which link ruler to ruled, centre to periphery and superior to subordinate are often depicted as patron-client relations. Students of African affairs seem more and more convinced that these relations are central to a proper understanding of African politics because it is through such relations that precarious regimes acquire a degree of structure and stability. (8) Patron-client relations are essentially forms of exchange relationship between unequals, relationships 'not only of mutual assistance and support, but also of recognised and accepted inequality between big men and lesser men' (Jackson and Roseberg,

1982, p. 39). Such relationships are reciprocal in that the form of support patrons need from their clients are only forthcoming when patrons supply the kinds of assistance demanded by their clients. The relationship is unequal because differences in status, income and power mean that 'the patron's need of an individual client is appreciably less than the individual client's need of a patron' (Hodder-Williams, 1985, p. 145).

Where regimes lack legitimacy, stability depends largely on the ability to secure loyalty and support through patron-client networks. Patronage becomes, in effect, a substitute for both ideological indoctrination and coercion. In the same way, patron-client relationships also serve to defuse discontent and channel political and economic demands through clientelist networks often of an ethnic or regional kind. Thus, clientelism, like corruption, is profoundly conservative and 'both serves as a mechanism for maintaining ruling class interests and, at the same time, systematically inhibits the articulation of class as a source of overt political conflict' (Clapham, 1985, p. 58).

But there is often an element of instability associated with patron-client networks which derives partly from factional competition among patrons and partly from the difficulty of meeting client aspirations from a stagnant or diminishing pool of patronage and other political resources. In the longer term, it is possible that clientelism may succumb to the impact of different forms of political and economic change. If Brownsberger and others are correct and significant 'development' occurs, the services currently provided by patrons will be in less demand, but if Africa's economic situation deteriorates further, many clients will tend to lose faith in the capacity of patrons to deliver. In the former case, the patron becomes redundant but, in the latter, he is threatened by potentially revolutionary upheaval. (9)

One problem with clientelism is that 'itself a form of corruption, it encourages corruption in other ways' and in particular 'it lends itself to a form of government by hand-out, in which the government itself becomes dependent on the sources of funds through which it is effectively obliged to buy support' (Clapham, 1985, p. 59). Whether the dependence is based on extracting surpluses from the peasantry, on foreign aid or on royalty payments from multinational corporations, the regime is unable to consider policy changes which would threaten financially its political supporters. Thus, if clientelism promotes a modicum of stability through the creation of networks of support, it also serves as a powerful brake on political and economic change. There is little doubt that clientelism is not only an important factor in African politics, but also a significant obstacle in controlling corruption. Regimes based largely on patronage and patron-client networks are often, even necessarily, corrupt and their survival impedes the task of creating political and economic conditions conducive to Weberian bureaucracy.

But, despite its obvious importance, care should be taken not to exaggerate the role of clientelism. Caution should be exercised because, like corruption, the concept of clientelism is elusive and is used to describe relationships of widely differing kinds.   There is no easy answer to the question, when is a patron-client relationship not a patron-client relationship? They vary, for example in scale, purpose, intensity, durability and exclusiveness. They lack discrete boundaries and, in consequence, their amorphous character makes it difficult to determine membership.   Because patron-client networks lack the formal organisation of, for example, a political party, there is always the possibility that such relationships may exist only in the minds of third parties. This is not to deny that the perception of such networks by other political actors may have important consequences, but to caution that the existence of such networks should not be a matter solely of faith. A further analytical difficulty is presented by the fact that the client of one patron may also be the client of another while, at different levels, individuals may simultaneously perform the roles of patron and client.

If clientelism is a feature of political life in many African countries, it would not be accurate to describe all African states as clientelist states. In Zaire, for example, corruption is pervasive, but much of it derives from sources other than patron-client relationships.   To utilise clientelism to characterise a national political style is to assert that patron-client relationships are more widespread and comprehensive than perhaps they are and there must always be some 'doubt whether any large political system can ever be described exclusively or even mainly by means of a clientelist model' (Lande, 1982, p. 9). In practice, formal organisational structures and clientelist networks are interwoven and the dominance of the latter over the former is neither guaranteed nor constant. Clientelism and the networks it generates both contribute to the spread of corruption and impede efforts to control it, but this is neither to claim that corruption and clientelism are synonymous nor to argue that either is a sufficient condition for the other.

To set out the conditions and circumstances likely to retard the growth of corruption or to describe the factors conducive to its reduction is to highlight the very qualities, advantages and characteristics which are most conspicuous by their absence in many African states.   Conversely, to construct a model of the political and economic factors which most facilitate the institutionalisation of corrupt practices is to identify some of the most prominent features of African political life.

If African bureaucracies fail to discharge their duties in accordance with Weberian expectations of integrity and efficiency, it is because there is little or no correspondence between Weber's assumptions and the prevailing political and economic circumstances of most African states. Weber's remarks on the attributes of bureaucracy were made subject to a number of conditions, most notably that officials are paid adequate and regular salaries, that there is effective supervision of subordinates and that sufficient training is given to ensure technical competence. Underlying the specific conditions, the broader assumptions are that the polity is stable, the economy soundly based, and that government revenues are secured by an established system of taxation.

The salaries of African officials, as we have seen, may be thought generous unless one considers the demands made on them by relatives, friends and communities. What would be more than adequate to support a nuclear family often proves inadequate for an extended one. But it would be wrong to assume that all bureaucrats face the problem of how to disburse their apparently large salaries because, in many countries, the monthly pay cheque is always 'in the post'. If customs officers have not been paid for several months, it is hardly surprising to find that they engage in a little private enterprise. According to Weber, the fact that bureaucrats enjoy job security means that they are less likely to demand greater remuneration, but African officials unlike, their expatriate predecessors, have never been able to look to the future with confidence. If they escape periodic purges and changes of regime, the bankruptcy of many regimes and rapid inflation precludes the possibility of a secure retirement and a steady pension. The consequence is that African bureaucrats operate with shorter time horizons than their Western counterparts and they have powerful incentives to exploit the fruits of office while they last.

The hierarchical principles of Weberian bureaucracy provide for the supervision of each layer of officials by a higher one but, while low-level corruption may be minimised by vigilant superiors, there is no guarantee that the higher levels will be alert, competent or honest. If corruption permeates the highest levels of a bureaucratic structure, attempts to eradicate it lower down the hierarchy are likely to be symbolic and attempts to combat it at the top can only come from external sources.

The pressure for public employment in Africa might suggest that it would be relatively easy to appoint competent staff. But this supposes both that educational opportunities and standards are good and that the recruitment process is designed to evaluate technical competence. In practice, educational standards are often low and recruitment is subject to party patronage, patron-client influences, nepotism and bribery. (10) The consequences, as we saw in the Nigerian oil corporation case, is that there is often a severe shortage of skilled and qualified personnel, most notably, accountants and auditors.

When officials are incompetent, inadequately supervised and subject to diverse financial pressures, they do not often display the attributes Weber anticipated. When the polity is unstable, the economy underdeveloped and tax revenues insufficient and erratic, the prospects for a smoothly operating administrative machine seem bleak. But it is not just the case that the pre-conditions for Weber's ideal-type are largely missing in Africa because there are other relevant requirements which Weber neglected to mention. In particular, the workload of officials must not be excessive and there should be some mechanism for the redress of grievances. As Clarke observes, 'where pay and competence are inadequate, workloads too high, supervision lax and complaints ineffective, modern bureaucracies cannot function, and are necessarily adapted along the lines of particularistic and political pressures' (Clarke (ed), 1983, p. xi).

In the conditions prevailing in modern Africa, corruption is difficult to evade, let alone control. The chronic shortages of consumer goods and the limited access to educational and employment opportunities mean that playing by the rules is to invite failure and disappointment. In some cases, if it were not for corruption, the black market and smuggling, the basic necessities of life would be effectively unobtainable. No doubt impersonal rule following has a role but 'it is asking a great deal of the ordinary man to expect him to sacrifice his personal well-being for some nebulous public goal' (Cartwright, 1983, p. 217). In states which possess no National Health Service, those who can afford it take out private medical insurance. Similarly, where states are unable or unwilling to provide economic security for their people, those who can afford it buy security through corruption. In other words, corruption is often the only available strategy which 'affords one a workable way of looking after one's needs and interests and achieving income and security' (Jackson and Rosberg, 1982, p. 45). (11) Trying to control corruption, without changing the conditions which generate and sustain it, is like trying to change a car wheel when the vehicle is still moving; the remedial effort is overwhelmed by the momentum of the larger body of which the wheel is an integral part. Conversely, where corruption inflicts serious economic damage, the wheel may come off anyway and the political regime, so to speak, runs off the road.

African experience suggests that it is always easier to detect and punish the corruption of one's political predecessors and opponents than it is to curb the activities of one's associates and supporters. It further suggests that, because of administrative weaknesses, economic constraints, external interference and the precarious domestic political standing of many regimes, the prospects of any regime being able to initiate and sustain a programme of fundamental reform directed at reducing inequality and corruption are far from bright. It is not so much the case that Africa lacks a supply of puritans as the fact that attempts to reconstruct societies damage vested interests. Few regimes possess the political will to attack such interests, the administrative capacity to sustain any such attack or the popular support to resist the inevitable counter-attack.

While the Afro-Marxist and some socialist states strive to limit the private accumulation of wealth, they are beset by difficulties and are sometimes willing to accept a degree of external direction of their economic affairs. Two Afro-Marxist states, Benin and Congo-Brazzaville, have chosen to belong to the CFA franc system because 'this compromise of autonomy averts the more disabling trauma of an inconvertible currency, with the inflation, shortages and smuggling this is likely to create' (Young, 1982, p.310). If such compromises are inevitable and, in practice, serve to maintain the political and economic order, it must be recognised that they also tend to exclude reforms which threaten either French interests or even the possibly corrupt activities of some French companies.

If the Afro-Marxist states struggle against the odds to curb corruption, some of the capitalist states are ready to spare themselves the anguish. In the more extreme cases, such as Zaire and Nigeria, capitalist values together with extensive privatisation of public resources have produced corruption on such a scale that it is difficult to see how the situation can be improved. If the structure and direction of corruption varies in Zaire and Nigeria, it only helps to demonstrate that there is more than one route to hell. To ask, for example, why the Kenyan government does not curb the activities of the Wabenzi is to mistake the criminal for the policeman. There seems little doubt that the African capitalist state displays such vulnerability to large-scale corruption that there is a distinct danger of it becoming, in Young's apt phrase, 'not the night watchman of classical liberalism but the brazen burglar' (1982, p. 308). The burglar can afford to be brazen when the guardians of the law are either unwilling to enforce it or are even prepared to change it to condone misconduct as, for example, when President Kenyatta amended the Kenyan constitution in 1975 to allow him to pardon KANU M.Ps convicted of electoral fraud.

Most African states are characterised by gross inequalities, not just the familiar economic inequalities of extremes of poverty and wealth, but inequalities of power. The centrality of the state in economic affairs, the prohibition or persecution of political opposition and widespread media censorship help produce and sustain an institutionalised inequality of power. The result is that the governors have little or no accountability to the governed and, the military aside, there seem to be no obvious sources of countervailing power. This situation leads to the anomaly of the least democratic organisation in any society, the armed forces, intervening in the political process ostensibly on behalf of the 'people'. But whether the government is civilian or military, political power is concentrated rather than dispersed and the people are expected to obey rather than participate. As we have seen, some military regimes even transpose military principles into the political arena and strive to 'discipline' their civilian populations.

If the ruled have little or no control over their rulers, then the control of corruption can only be achieved by members of the political elite themselves. But even where a sizeable proportion of the elite is not personally or blatantly corrupt, their political positions often depend on their continuing ability to channel resources and favours to their clients and associates. This means, for example, that it is extremely likely that the regulatory, 'neo-mercantalist' role of so many states will continue because it guarantees access to essential political resources. Factional competition among patrons and the constant need to bolster lines of political support suggest that the ability of individual members of an elite to play the political game by different rules is extremely limited. The art of political leadership in Africa often consists in the careful balancing of contending factions and the resources of the state are indispensable instruments for maintaining political equilibrium. Thus, when the future of the leader and his regime is at stake, the political implications of exposing corruption have to be weighed carefully. Factional competition means that 'while all condemn and abhor corruption and patronage, they tend to do so largely when they are practised by opponents' (Szeftel in Clarke (ed), 1983, p. 179).

Purges, codes of conduct, deterrent sentencing and wars against indiscipline may suggest that the political leadership is sincerely striving to reduce levels of corruption. They may also suggest that the leadership is using the corruption issue to pick off its opponents and to undermine or deter potential challenges to its power. They may even suggest that popular discontent has reached such proportions that it is time to sacrifice some victims on the altar of public opinion. As most political leaders appreciate, focusing attention on the misdeeds of individuals helps deflect public concern away from the structures and mechanisms which generate the opportunities for corruption.

This is not to suggest that the measures employed against corruption are always entirely inconsequential. Impressionistically, it seems that the six months of Murtala Mohammed's rule in Nigeria in 1976 had a relatively dramatic impact on both the incidence of corruption and public attitudes towards it. It is also possible that the public executions in Ghana and Liberia had a similar short-term impact. But it is not clear how even a forceful personality like Murtala Mohammed could sustain his immediate success without resolving Nigeria's formidable political, administrative and economic problems. In the event, of course, both the reduction of corruption and the regime itself were short-lived.

The control of corruption in Africa ultimately depends on the political will of Africa's leaders and on the capacity of their governments to implement their policies. But both political will and administrative capacity are intimately related to the different kinds of economic policies which governments pursue and their differential societal consequences. Too often, personal, partisan and factional considerations inhibit or eliminate the possibility of effective action. Too often, there is a gulf between an austere and puritanical leader or leadership group and the wider political elite. Clearly, political leaders must set an example if they expect to reduce levels of corruption, but merely setting a personal example is by no means sufficient when it also involves condoning the activities of associates and subordinates who manipulate the power of the state to create private fortunes.

African economies have displayed an enduring inability to meet the basic needs, let alone the material aspirations of their populations, and continuing shortages and bottlenecks increase pressures on consumers to seek corrupt solutions to their economic problems. While there is, admittedly, considerable scope for improvement in economic policy-making in Africa, a large part of Africa's economic destiny is decided elsewhere. Decisions made in Accra may be nullified by the activities of commodity brokers in London, while choices made in Maputo may be counteracted by decisions made in Pretoria. But this is to assume that economic decision-makers are concerned with the general or public interest of their societies. In practice, decision-making is often designed to further private rather than public interests, to reward already privileged groups rather than to alleviate poverty. Such tendencies are exacerbated by the efforts of multinational corporations to corrupt officials dealing with the export of capital and the awarding of contracts, licences and franchises. Such corporations are generally either concerned with extracting raw materials from Africa or with selling goods to the urban elite. The lack of purchasing and political power of the peasant majority means there is little incentive for the domestic political elite or their foreign business associates to change economic direction.

This chapter has been concerned to demonstrate that the control of corruption cannot be viewed as an isolated, discrete problem which is readily susceptible to improved management techniques, intensified ethical instruction, or military-style discipline. Obviously, there is scope for improvement in bureaucratic procedures and training, especially those involving accounting and the award of contracts, but to imagine that administrative reform alone will solve the problem is an illusion. In too many cases, the problem is a non-problem in that far from attempting to improve the situation, governments, or at least major parts of them, are the problem. Anti-corruption campaigns then degenerate into political rhetoric designed more to appease foreign donors and international finance institutions than to address the major issues. In other cases, intractable economic and security problems, as in Angola and Mozambique, mean that more radical anti-corruption measures are less effective than their authors sometimes claim.

If 'development' seems to hold the key to corruption, its achievement and precise nature are still problematic. The competing claims of the socialist command economy or the capitalist market economy have yet to be properly tested. Such testing is unlikely to occur while the 'neo-mercantalist' state with its extensive economic regulation still produces political and material benefits for those who control the administrative machine. The immediate prospects for radical change in Africa seem poor but, without it, it seems likely that ideologists will continue to peddle their patent remedies, politicians and soldiers will continue to preach and to purge and corruption will continue to flourish.

NOTES

(1)   Analyses of Tanzanian politics which focus on the concept of class struggle (Shivji, 1976) explain curbs on the entrepreneurial activities of public officials and politicians in terms of a conflict between the managerial and commercial fractions of the bourgeoisie.

(2)   Corruption is not only hard to prove, but charges of corruption are not easy to refute. Where governments dismiss such charges as mischievous, they may be accused of covering up; where they establish inquiries which find no compelling evidence, there are accusations of 'whitewash'. If corruption is popularly perceived as prevalent, all public officials are likely to be presumed guilty and the occasional, scandal merely confirms the validity of the 'iceberg' theory.

(3)   Rawlings' severity is not merely retrospective because offences committed during his regime have also been harshly punished. In May, 1985, two bank officials were executed for their part in a fraud on the Ghana Commercial bank. See (Africa Research Bulletin, June 15, 1985, p. 7652).

(4)   Where avenues of promotion are blocked, the temptation to write anonymous letters accusing senior officials of corruption may be hard to resist. If senior officials are corrupt, self-advancement and public duty happily coincide.

(5)   The unpopularity and authoritarianism of Major-General Idiagbon and WAI are thought to be two of the reasons behind the 'palace coup' of August, 27th, 1985, in which Major-General Babangida replaced Major-General Buhari as head of state. Neither Buhari nor Idiagbon have a place on the new ruling military council.

(6)   Reporting the failures of the bureaucratic state in Africa is easier than exploring and explaining such failures, but see (Brett, 1985) for a perceptive discussion of the issues.

(7)   If rapid growth is often characterised by breakdowns in auditing procedures, stock control and in state purchasing systems, recession and austerity frequently involve salary restrictions and tight import controls. Thus, while growth multiplies opportunities, recession may sharpen incentives. In 'boom' times, corruption may be one avenue to wealth but, in depression days, it may be the only one.

(8)   The complexities and varieties of patron-client relations are fully discussed in (Clapham (ed), 1982; and Schmidt et al (eds), 1977).

(9)   It could, of course, be argued that, for many of the rural poor, revolutionary activity is scarcely a viable option. In such circumstances, even weak and ineffective patrons may retain their clients because the latter have no realistic alternative strategy to pursue.

(10)   Where there are ten candidates for every patronage appointment, there is always the danger that in making a choice, you create nine enemies and one ingrate.

(11)   Jackson and Rosberg should, more accurately, have said that corruption affords some a way of meeting their material needs. As always, the poorest members of society usually lack the resources to engage in corrupt transactions.

7 Conclusion

The major problem in explaining the role and significance of corruption is the extent to which it seems embedded or ingrained in African politics. If corruption is often likened to cancer, African experience suggests that it is a more serious form than skin cancer because it is less often an exceptional, superficial blemish or irritant than an integral, institutionalised feature of political and economic processes. In such circumstances, it is particularly difficult both to envisage how African politics would function without it and to trace the precise consequences of its presence.

Despite these difficulties, many observers believe that corruption is responsible for a variety of social, political and economic ills and, presumably, they believe that its elimination or reduction would, in some sense, prove beneficial. But the question of how important corruption is, what evil consequences it generates and the nature of the benefits its reduction would bring remain matters of contention. Some scholars see corruption as the cause of political and economic ills, others see it as both symptom and cause, while still others see it primarily as a symptom of larger processes of social change. Clearly, such views cannot all be true of all African states all the time, but it is certainly possible that, in different circumstances or at different times, differing perceptions of the role of corruption are appropriate. In other words, changing circumstances and varying contexts mean that the impact of corruption is neither uniform nor constant.

It therefore seems necessary to qualify what sometimes appears to be obviously and necessarily true, for example, it is often alleged that corruption is an inefficient method of using manpower and resources and that its growth undermines existing levels of administrative efficiency. But to say that corrupt polities do not possess the most efficient forms of administration is not to claim that, without corruption, African states would necessarily be more efficiently managed. (1) In some cases, as we have seen, corruption may be more a symptom of administrative inefficiency than its cause. It sometimes galvanises stagnant bureaucracies and provides officials with incentives to deliver services. Corruption can therefore offer a means of goading elements of the bureaucracy into action and, to that extent, it stimulates rather than impedes efficiency.

But it may be objected that if bureaucratic responsiveness is only available at a price, those without the means to pay are likely to be ignored. Furthermore, the neglect of the poor may be seen less as an unintended, if inevitable, consequence of corruption than as its central purpose. Corruption, in this view, necessarily involves 'the exclusion of those unable to participate in paying for corruptly given favours. Its essential objective is to eliminate competition, to create a charmed circle, an inside track. As such it is profoundly anti-democratic' (Clarke (ed), 1983, p.xvi). (2) If corruption is undemocratic because it excludes the poorer sections of African societies from access to public goods and services, it also seems to create further inequalities by transferring wealth from society at large to particular groups or sections within it.

In political terms, corruption is sometimes held responsible for exacerbating factional conflict and thereby encouraging political instability, for subverting the ends of government policy and, ultimately, for undermining the legitimacy of the political system. If political activity in Africa is primarily concerned with the acquisition and retention of state power, corruption is sometimes seen as an obstacle to its exercise because it has 'corrosive effects on trust in public authorities, and hence on their capacity to direct communal action towards the achievement of common goals' (Clapham 1985, p.54). In the course of this study, we have seen ample evidence to support such charges but, given the earlier warnings about variety and diversity, it should not be supposed that such charges can always or necessarily be substantiated.

Corruption is, in some cases, as much a scapegoat as an explanation for Africa's ills. It may heighten factional conflict, but it does not seem to create it. It may delay or distort the implementation of government policies, but delays and distortions are common without corruption. Admittedly, it is hard to see how, in general terms, corruption can contribute to the legitimacy of a political system, but to claim that it corrodes it is to

assume that many African regimes have a significant degree of
legitimacy to lose. As we have seen, one of the major problems
in controlling corruption is that governments in Africa are
frequently perceived as alien, oppressive and unaccountable. The
orderly transfer of power through a mechanism of 'free and fair'
competitive elections is, of course, very much the exception to
the rule in African politics. The centrality of the state in
African economies means that the urge to acquire, maintain and
exploit public office is extremely powerful. Thus, the rewards of
political and bureaucratic success are enormous, while the costs of
failure are very heavy. In such contexts, it is extremely unlikely
that the participants in the political struggle will have much
recourse to the Marquis of Queensbury's rules.

The underlying conditions which shape the activities of African
polities are so inhospitable and intractable that, corruption or
not,there is likely to be acute and widespread competition for the
grossly inadequate and, at best, stagnant pool of public resources.
It is not realistic, therefore, to imagine that there is some kind
of choice to be made between a corrupt bureaucracy and a
Weberian one, between the unseemly factional scramble for
patronage and favours and the more disciplined contest of
ideologically distinct parliamentary parties, or between corruption
and poverty and integrity and prosperity. Corruption may be
anti-democratic, but then African societies display a variety of
other features which militate against both the inculcation of
democratic values and the development of democratic structures.

Parliamentary democracies, like Weberian bureaucracies, emerge
and survive in political and economic environments that are
largely alien to the African experience. Constitutional documents,
like organisation charts, provide pathetically flimsy paper defences
against the urgent imperatives of political and bureaucratic
survival.When politics and bureaucracy are but two roads among
many to fame and fortune, defeat and disappointment are more
readily tolerated than when they provide the only avenues of
personal advancement. If the political will to tackle the issue of
corruption is often missing, its presence is rarely sufficient to
overcome the variety of domestic and external pressures and
constraints which beset so many African regimes. A   political
leadership which is unable to provide an adequate supply of basic
necessities to its country's population, which has little or no
legitimacy in the eyes of its people and which does not possess
skilled and loyal administrative subordinates is imperfectly
prepared to combat corruption. Unfortunately, a large number of
African states currently suffer from these and other important
deficiencies and there are few prospects of early improvement.

But if corruption seems likely to resist all symbolic and most
substantive efforts to eliminate it, it may be useful to consider

whether its consequences are as pernicious as some observers have claimed. In certain circumstances, the most likely alternatives to corruption may be even more unpalatable, for example, if bureaucratic corruption is thought to derive largely from inadequate salaries, one obvious remedy is to raise them, but this would probably necessitate a general and intolerable increase in the tax burden. It might even be argued that, far from being 'anti-democratic' or conservative in its intent, corruption is sometimes progressive and serves to widen rather than narrow access to the political arena. If the bribe process is restricted to those who can afford it, the poor only suffer if it can be shown that, without bribery, their prospects of obtaining particular public goods would have been significantly better. But when goods, services and jobs are in such chronically short supply and the demand is so large that nearly all applicants are going to be disappointed, corruption has no direct material impact on the lives of the overwhelming majority. Similarly, where groups are excluded from access to public services or benefits on, for example, racial or religious grounds, corruption may supply one means of integrating them into the political system. (3)

But if the poor do not directly 'suffer' from corruption, it can scarcely be argued that it does anything to assist them. If their material prospects remain, in reality, largely unaffected, corruption may still reduce further their commitment to the political system by exacerbating disillusionment and encouraging attempts to 'exit'. In practice, the peasantry may be paying twice for some services, once through taxation and marketing board price manipulation and once through corruption. Similarly, far from increasing bureaucratic salaries and the consequent tax burden, it may be thought more desirable to ease the financial pressures on the peasantry by reducing the size and the salaries of the bureaucracy.

In conditions of underdevelopment, with their attendant shortages and paucity of resources, corruption tends mostly to accentuate and aggravate the political and economic inequalities which have characterised so many African states for so long. It has been argued in this book that the form and incidence of corruption in any African country is largely a product of its political and economic history and, while it has been possible to identify some common constraints, it has also been necessary to point out that political ideology, policy choices and individual personalities do make a difference. It is also important to point out that incorruptible leadership, prudent policy choices and a coherent ideological doctrine do not provide cast iron protection from the growth of corruption. The economic and political destinies of African regimes are only partially under their control because they are prone to external political and economic manipulation deriving either from powerful or hostile neighbours like South Africa or from other attempts to extend or maintain foreign influence. (4)

Political corruption on the scale practised in modern Africa is not an alien virus parachuted in to infect the body politic. It spreads and grows within political systems in forms and patterns which reflect both the extent to which political leaders lack a sense of purpose or direction and their consequent failure to 'link society and government in a shared sense of values' (Clapham, 1985, p. 54). Widespread corruption does not suddenly appear or disappear overnight. It develops over time where environmental conditions are congenial and its rate of growth can be accelerated by major changes in particular environments, for example, the oil boom in Nigeria in the 1970s.

Despite its relative brevity, the colonial period, as we have seen, made an enduring contribution in creating the conditions hospitable to the growth of corruption. Collaboration with colonial authorities brought, in many cases, access to new forms of wealth, status and power. In other instances, the imposition of colonial rule forced chiefs and other local rulers to act as major agents of social change in areas such as tax collection, policing and recruiting wage labour for colonial projects. In Nigeria and Kenya, one result was that 'Ibo and Kikuyu chiefs played a major role in undercutting local political and economic self-sufficiency and mobilising human and material resources for colonial exploitation' (Tignor, 1971 p.347). But whether the tasks which fell to local rulers are regarded as opportunities or impositions, such rulers had to develop their own coercive and administrative apparatus to perform them. One historian has concluded that, without corruption, 'the whole system would have collapsed, for the vast para-administrative and military organisation had to be created and financed. Thus chiefs were compelled to exact what colonial governments regarded as "illegal tribute" from local populations' (Tignor, 1971, p.351). If the chiefs recruited or conscripted by the colonial authorities became, in the eyes of their effective employers, 'corrupt', they were similarly viewed by their own people because their impositions lacked the credibility of tradition and their authority rested less on reciprocal relationships and more on coercion.

Colonialism created new social hierarchies based on racial superiority and established new central authorities which distorted customary relationships and served as inspiration and model for aspiring individuals. If local leaders were required, in a sense, to do the 'dirty work' for their colonial masters by conscripting labour and extracting tax revenues, it seems likely that they would shift the main burdens away from their families and supporters. Control of local political institutions then provided not only a means of personal enrichment, but a method of allocating the impositions of colonial rule in unfair and uneven ways. In consequence, the contentious distribution of burdens tended both to intensify local rivalries and antagonisms and to inculcate the attitude that one man's gain is another man's loss.

From such a perspective, government and its administrative opportunities became the ultimate prize and politics the means to its achievement. This tendency to personal, local or regional competition and rivalry was, of course, reinforced by the restrictions colonial authorities placed on the formation of wider political groupings and by the obstacles of language, literacy, finance and communications. In the extreme case, countries like Nigeria were manufactured from colonial territories which had not only been separate entities, but which had been governed on very different principles. In such circumstances, the antagonism, jealousy and suspicion characteristic of the Nigerian federation since its inception was not wholly unexpected.

If the political impact of colonial rule was partly to encourage local, regional and factional forms of political competition based on 'zero-sum' views of the political process, equally important inheritances were the assumptions and attitudes characteristic of hierarchical and authoritarian forms of government. With such political legacies, it is scarcely surprising that ideological cohesion, governmental accountability and disinterested bureaucracies remain, at best, elusive aspirations.

While the political legacies of colonial rule were clearly substantial, the economic effects played an even more important role in shaping environments conducive to the growth of corruption. Some economic effects were direct and immediate, for example, the loss of land and livelihood in settler colonies and the consequent expansion in wage employment. These and other enforced changes in African patterns of agricultural production and subsistence necessarily distorted established social, political and economic relationships and accentuated socio-economic differentiation. But although such developments were to have important political consequences, colonial regulation of commerce and business and, more particularly, the limitations placed on African participation in these areas, served both to inhibit the growth of an indigenous bourgeois class and to concentrate African attention on alternative careers in politics and bureaucracy. If private avenues were blocked by racial discrimination and shortages of capital, the established hierarchies of the government apparatus provided the only other feasible ladder of upward mobility.

Not only did nationalist politics and bureaucratic employment provide vehicles for African ambition but, on independence, they provided crucial access to sources of patronage and wealth. The

coercive and exploitive character of colonial rule was, in many
cases, readily adapted to the purposes of the new African
leadership groups who sought, for the most part, to perpetuate the
privileges enjoyed by their European predecessors. Entrepreneurial
Africans unable to find a suitable niche within the governmental
apparatus often found useful and lucrative employment as
intermediaries, agents and brokers between the public and private
sectors of the economy. The centrality of the state in colonial
Africa ensured that subsequent political and economic competition
would focus on acquiring possession of, or access to, public
resources. But the fruits of victory were so sweet and the
alternatives so bleak, it was almost inevitable that the
competition for, and conduct of, public office would assume
corrupt forms. The expansion of the bureaucratic state in
post-colonial times ostensibly to tackle the problems of
development has, in many cases, simply multiplied the
opportunities for corruption. This is apparent in, for example, the
proliferation of marketing bodies and parastatal
organisations. Thus while the distortions of African economic
development introduced by colonial rule provided compelling
incentives to engage in corrupt activity, the centralised,
authoritarian structure of the state provided ample opportunities
to extort funds from the productive sectors of the economy.

The form corruption actually takes in Africa clearly depends on
a variety of factors including the structure and openness of the
economy, the limitations on political competition and criticism,
and the institutional characteristics of the government.
Corruption, as we have seen, pursues discretionary power and its
absence may signify administrative impotence rather than
integrity. Political institutions in Africa sometimes survive in a
formal or symbolic sense long after they have been by-passed or
stripped of effective power and, while the main arena of
corruption is always the discretionary power of the state, the
institutional expression of these powers differs from time to time
and place to place. All bureaucracies share a commitment to
hierarchy and the division of functions, but different operating
procedures, circumstances and clientele help ensure that the
structure of corruption varies from state to state. There does not
appear to be any clear or compelling evidence to suggest that one
form of bureaucratic organisation is less or more likely to
generate corruption than any other. If administrative
centralisation concentrates power and thereby increases the
incentive to offer corrupt inducements, decentralisation disperses
power, multiplies the points of access to government resources and
thereby increases the opportunities for corrupt transactions. Thus,
the structural characteristics of an African bureaucracy seem
more likely to guide corruption along particular channels or
through particular mechanisms than to impede or accelerate its
general progress.

If students of corruption have found it analytically useful to distinguish between different types or levels of corruption, for example, between incidental, systematic and systemic corruption or between bribery and extortion, it should be noted that such distinctions are, in practice, always difficult, often arbitrary and sometimes unhelpful. In particular, it is hard to delineate the boundaries between such forms and thus the clarity and utility of the distinctions are called into question. It is one thing to argue that punishing individuals who receive bribes fails to address the problem of what causes bribery, and quite another to advocate an individualistic emphasis where extortion is involved. When Clarke asserts, in regard to extortion, 'Eliminate the corrupt entrepreneur and you eliminate the corruption, since it is from him that the impetus comes' (1983, p.xv), he seems curiously uninterested in discovering why the corrupt entrepreneur behaves as he does. If extortion is necessary to lubricate the mechanisms of political support, the removal of one corrupt entrepreneur is likely to prove a very temporary palliative. Admittedly, in the extreme case of a Mobutu or Acheampong, the benefits may be slightly more durable and tangible but, for the most part, Clarke's distinction between bribery and extortion seems to depend on the unjustified assumption that the former is socially or structurally determined while the latter is the work of 'bad men'.

The problem of distinguishing between different types or levels of corruption in Africa is exacerbated by the extent to which political relationships generally are coloured by considerations of private or partisan advantage and the consequent lack of agreement on, or commitment to, rules of public conduct. However defined, corruption is an important element in the governmental processes of many African countries but, if it is possible and desirable to isolate it for examination, it should be stressed that, in practice, it commonly forms part of a broader pattern or style of political activity and it is the particular pattern or style which gives corruption its meaning and significance. In spoils systems or 'neo-patrimonial' systems, the function of corruption is clearly different from its role in polities where conflict is channelled and regulated by legitimate popular institutions and effective legal processes.

In many African states, corruption exists within political contexts or climates which support and encourage personalism, factionalism, patronage and patron-client relationships. In such contexts, governments may systematically favour members of particular parties, regions and ethnic groups or shape public policies to perpetuate or promote the advantages of privileged elites. In practice, they often do both and, in such circumstances, exaggerated anxiety about the level of corruption seems misplaced and slightly suspicious. If many African leaders wring their hands in anguish because so many of their officials flout civil service rules and regulations, it can scarcely be denied that, at the highest levels, there are often no effective rules governing the conduct of public office.

Africa's political rulers rarely recognise procedural or legal constraints on their power and, in the circumstances, it does not seem surprising either that their subordinates should seek a similar freedom of conduct or that attempts to improve political and administrative mechanisms should often fail conspicuously. The Nigerian Constitution of 1979 was explicitly modelled on the United States Constitution but, regrettably, legal and institutional reforms do not always travel well. Medical transplants are fraught with difficulty in the most favourable circumstances but, when there is no compatibility or similarity between donor and recipient, the prospects are poor. Despite its wealth, strength and stability, the United States has not always lived up to the ideal of 'a government of laws and not of men'. The outlook for impoverished, insecure and unstable Africa is infinitely worse. (5)

If Madison was right when he argued that the main difficulty in framing a government is that 'you must first enable the government to control the governed, and in the next place oblige it to control itself' (Hamilton, Madison and Jay, Federalist, No. 51, 1961), it seems clear that African governments labour under multiple handicaps. They possess such limited capacities for administrative implementation and political mobilisation that they are often unable to carry through policy decisions requiring more than simple, short-term coercion. More generally, they clearly often lack the financial, material, technical and human resources to develop levels of political control and support sufficient to produce and sustain substantial programmes of economic and social change.

The effective impotence of the state is partly disguised or camouflaged by the weakness or even absence of countervailing forces or organisations. In most cases, political competition takes place almost entirely within the ruling civilian or military faction. Other forms of competition are precluded or discouraged by coercing or co-opting potential opponents, by creating one-party states, by emasculating or absorbing trade unions and professional organisations and by controlling or harassing the press. Even in Nigeria, a country with a long and vigorous history of press freedom, editors and journalists recently found themselves in prison for publishing articles which allegedly brought discredit on the Buhari regime. (6) If civilian regimes face the prospect of military intervention, challenges to military regimes are, as the overthrow of Buhari demonstrates, largely internal rather than external. But it is wrong to assume that military intervention necessarily or even commonly represents a threat to the material interests of the privileged sections of African societies. The radical, reforming soldier is the exception to the rule and, for much of the time, the military are appeased by appealing to their own corporate and material interests.

To the harassed African journalist or academic, the state can appear all-powerful but, to a foreign power or a transnational corporation, it can seem fragile, vulnerable and impotent. If political corruption is identified as an important feature of the post-colonial state, it is rarely a dominant one. Corruption seems to reflect rather than determine the character of political activity in Africa and perceptions of corruption need to be reconciled with our understanding of how the modern African state came into being, how it functions and what limits constrain its future development. But perceptions of corruption in Africa are often based on misconceptions and therefore this study has sought to chart the growth of corruption, to explore its various forms, to investigate its association with different types of regime and to assess the difficulties connected with its reduction.

The task has proved formidable, not merely because of the author's limitations, but because the issues are inherently complex. If satisfactory explanations of corruption in Africa continue to prove elusive, it should at least be clear that 'bad men' and good intentions are only a part of the story. Admittedly, Africa has suffered voracious predators like Amin and Acheampong, but it has also produced a Nyerere and a Rawlings. This is not to suggest that corrupt polities can often be rescued by brave leaders because, even where the political spirit is willing, the state and economy are usually weak. Too often in Africa, the political will and commitment to tackle corruption is in doubt and Madison's optimistic belief that governments can be made to control themselves seems sadly misplaced.

NOTES

(1)   Although this is a large subject, it is important to note here that, in any bureaucracy, the formal legal framework is given life by the existence of informal norms, groups and understandings. It is also important to remember that control and accountability, rather than innovation and development, are the priorities of Weberian type bureaucracies. One implication is that no single administrative form or style is guaranteed to be efficient and effective in all circumstances for all purposes. In particular situations, a high level of ideological commitment among senior officials may serve to provide a degree of immunity from corruption as well as strengthening attempts to mobilise and transform underdeveloped societies. Where political opposition is

prohibited or discouraged, administrative neutrality is likely to be seen as inappropriate or even disloyal.

The literature on organisational structure and behaviour is extensive but (Merton et al (eds), 1952 Hill, 1972; and Dunsire, 1973) discuss the salient issues.

(2) Clarke seems to equate democracy with equal access to government resources but, by this standard, most 'democracies' are, to varying degrees, undemocratic. Democracy is popularly associated with the principle of majority rule, but majority rule does not guarantee equal access for minorities as Ulster Catholics, black Americans and East African Asians would testify. Where religious or racial exclusion is linked to economic deprivation, the opportunities to utilise corrupt channels are correspondingly diminished.

(3) Lebanese or Asian businessmen and other 'pariah capitalists' often find that corruption more than compensates for their lack of citizen status and their exclusion from formal political and administrative channels. Where access and influence can be purchased, the flow of reciprocal benefits helps ensure a degree of commitment to regime stability.

(4) It is difficult to envisage how the governments of, for example, Angola and Mozambique can effectively pursue their political and social goals while South Africa's vested interest in their continued destabilisation remains so high. In such cases, corruption can be an instrument of external manipulation.

(5) If successful transplants require the matching of types, Nigeria and the United States do not immediately spring to mind as possessing close political, economic and cultural affinities. This is not, of course, to preclude the possibility of some sort of federal solution to the problems of governing such a large and diverse country, but rather to question whether institutional reforms alone are likely to make a serious impact on levels of corruption.

(6) When Major-General Babangida overthrew Buhari in August 1985, he quickly ordered the release of detained journalists and repealed the unpopular Decree No. 4 which had effectively proscribed criticism of Buhari's government.

References

The works listed below are those cited in the text and notes of this book. They do not constitute a bibliography though clearly many of them would find a place in a select bibliography of works on political corruption. Scholars working in this field are, inevitably, dependent on newspapers, magazines and other non-academic publications. A number of such publications are cited in the text, but particular mention should be made of West Africa as an invaluable research tool.

Abernethy, David B., 'Bureaucratic Growth and Economic Decline in Sub-Saharan Africa', paper to Africa Studies Association, Boston, 1983.

Abraham, Henry J., Freedom and the Court, Second Edition, Oxford University Press, New York, 1972.

Aina, S., 'Bureaucratic Corruption in Nigeria: The Continuing Search for Causes and Cures', International Review of Administrative Sciences, vol. XLVIII, no.1, 1982.

Almond, Gabriel A. and Coleman James S., (eds), The Politics of the Developing Areas, Princeton University Press, Princeton, New Jersey, 1960.

Anonymous Kenyan authors, Independent Kenya, Zed Press, London, 1982.

Apter, David E., Ghana in Transition, Atheneum, New York,

1963.

Austin, Dennis G., Politics in Ghana, 1946-1960, Oxford
    University Press, London, 1962.
Barkan, J.D., (ed), Politics and Public Policy in Kenya
    and Tanzania, Praeger, New York, 1979.
Barnett, D.L. and Njama, K., Mau Mau From Within, Monthly
    Review Press, New York, 1966.
Baylies, Carolyn L. and Szeftel, Morris, 'The Rise of a
    Zambian Capitalist Class in the 1970s', Journal of Southern
    African Studies, 8, no. 2, 1982.
Beattie, John, Other Cultures, Routledge and Kegan Paul,
    London, 1964.
Bendix, Reinhard, Max Weber, Methuen and Co., London, 1966
Bennell, P., 'The Colonial Legacy of Salary Structures in
    Anglophone Africa', Journal of Modern African Studies, 20, 1,
    1982.
Benson, George C.S., Political Corruption in America, D.C.
    Heath and Co., Lexington, 1978.
Berg, Larry L. et al. Corruption in the American Political
    System, General Learning Press, Morristown, 1976.
Bienen, Henry, Kenya: The Politics of Participation and
    Control, Princeton University Press, Princeton, New Jersey, 1974.
Blau, Peter, M. and Scott, W. Richard, Formal Organisations,
    Routledge and Kegan Paul, London, 1963.
Brett, E.A., Colonialism and Underdevelopment in East Africa,
    Heinemann, London, 1973.
Brett, E.A., 'State Power and Economic Inefficiency:
    Explaining Political Failure in Africa', paper to The Political
    Studies Association Conference, Manchester, 1985.
Brownsberger, W.N., 'Development and Governmental Corruption;
    Materialism and Political Fragmentation in Nigeria', Journal of
    Modern African Studies, vol. 21, no. 2, 1983.
Cartey, Wilfred and Kilson, Martin (eds), The Africa Reader;
    Colonial Africa, Random House, New York, 1970.
Cartwright, John, Political Leadership in Africa, Croom Helm,
    London, 1983.
Clapham, Christopher (ed), Private Patronage and Public Power:
    Political Clientelism in the Modern State, Frances Pinter,
    London, 1982.
Clapham, Christopher (ed), Third World Politics, Croom Helm,
    London, 1985.
Clarke, Michael (ed), Corruption: Causes, Consequences and
    Control, Frances Pinter, London, 1983.
Coleman, James S., Nigeria: Background to Nationalism,
    University of California Press, Berkeley, 1958.
Davidson, Basil, Africa in Modern History, Allen Lane, London,
    1978.
Dobel, J.P., 'The Corruption of a State', American Political
    Science Review, vol. 72, no. 3, 1978.
Doig, Alan, Corruption and Misconduct in Contemporary British

Politics, Penguin, London, 1984.
Dudley, Billy, _An Introduction to Nigerian Government and Politics_, Macmillan, London, 1982.
Dumont, Rene, _False Start in Africa_, Andre Deutsch, London, 1966.
Dunn, John (ed), _West African States: Failure and Promise_, Cambridge University Press, London, 1978.
Dunsire, Andrew, _Administration: The Word and the Science_, Martin Robertson, London, 1973.
Ekpo, M.U. (ed), _Bureaucratic Corruption in Sub-Saharan Africa_, University Press of America, Washington, D.C., 1979
Fanon, Franz, _The Wretched of the Earth_, Penguin, London, 1967
Fieldhouse, D.K., _The Colonial Empires: A Comparative Survey from the Eighteenth Century_, 2nd edn, Macmillan, London, 1982.
Frank, A.G., _Capitalism and Underdevelopment in Latin America_, Penguin Books, London, 1971.
Gertzel, Cherry et al (ed), _The dynamics of the one-party state in Zambia_, Manchester University Press, 1984.
Gould, D.J., _Bureaucratic Corruption and Underdevelopment: The Case of Zaire_, Pergamon Press, New York, 1980.
Grindle, Merilee S. (ed), _Politics and Policy Implementation in the Third World_, Princeton University Press, Princeton, New Jersey, 1980.
Hamilton, Alexander, Madison, James, Jay, John, _The Federalist Papers_, The New American Library, New York, 1961.
Harbeson, John W., _Nation Building in Kenya: The Role of Land Reform_, Northwestern University Press, Evanston, 1973.
Higgott, R.A., _Political Development Theory_, Croom Helm, London, 1983.
Hill, Michael J., _The Sociology of Public Administration_, Weidenfeld and Nicholson, London, 1972.
Hodder-Williams, Richard, _An Introduction to the Politics of Tropical Africa_, Allen and Unwin, London, 1984.
Hopkins, A.G., _An Economic History of West Africa_, Longman, London, 1973.
Huntington, Samuel P., _Political Order in Changing Societies_, Yale University Press, New Haven, 1968.
Isaacman, Allen and Isaacman, Barbara, _Mozambique: From Colonialism to Revolution, 1900-1982_, Westview Press, Boulder, Colorado, 1983.
Isichei, Elizabeth, _A History of Nigeria_, Longman, London, 1983.
Jackson, R.H. and Rosberg, C.J., _Personal Rule in Black Africa_, University of California Press, 1982.
Leff, Nathaniel, 'Economic Development Through Bureaucratic Corruption', _The American Behavioural Scientist_, 8, 1964.
LeVine, V., _Political Corruption: The Ghana Case_, Hoover Institution Press, Stanford, 1975.
Leys, Colin, _Underdevelopment in Kenya_, Heinemann, London, 1975.

Lyon, P. and Manor, J., (eds), Transfer and Transformation:
Political Institutions in the New Commonwealth, Leicester
University Press, 1983.

MacIntyre, Alasdair, Against the Self-Images of the Age:
Essays on Ideology and Philosophy, Duckworth, London, 1971.

Melson, Robert and Wolpe, Howard, (eds), Nigeria:
Modernization and the Politics of Communalism, Michigon State
University Press, 1971.

Merton, Robert K. et al (eds), Reader in Bureaucracy, The Free
Press, New York, 1952.

Mulford, David C., Zambia: The Politics of Independence
1957-1964, Oxford University Press, London, 1967.

Ndegwa, D.N., Report of the Commission of Inquiry (Public
Service Structure and Remunerations Commission), Government
Printer, Nairobi, 1971.

Olowu, D., 'The Nature of Bureaucratic Corruption in
Nigeria', International Review of Administrative Sciences, vol.
XLIX, no. 3, 1983.

Ottaway, David and Marina, Afrocommunism, Africana Publishing
Company, New York, 1981.

Panter-Brick, K. (ed), Soldiers and Oil, Frank Cass, London,
1978.

Peil, Margaret, Nigerian Politics: The Peoples View, Cassell,
London, 1976.

Rodney, Walter, How Europe Underdeveloped Africa,
Bogle-L'Ouverture Publications, London, 1972.

Rose-Ackerman, Susan, Corruption: A Study in Poltical Economy,
Academic Press, New York, 1978.

Rosberg, C.G. and Callaghy, T.M. (eds), Socialism in
Sub-Saharan Africa, University of California, Berkeley, 1979.

Rosberg, Carl G. Jr. and Nottingham, John, The Myth of 'Mau
Mau': Nationalism in Kenya, Praeger, New York, 1966.

Roxborough, Ian, Theories of Underdevelopment, Macmillan,
London, 1979.

Runciman, W.G., Social Science and Political Theory,
2nd. Edn., Cambridge University Press, 1969.

Schmidt, S.W. et al (eds), Friends, Followers and Factions: A
Reader in Political Clientelism, University of California Press,
1977.

Scott, James C., Comparative Political Corruption,
Prentice-Hall, New Jersey, 1972.

Scott, I., 'Political Money and Party Organisation in Zambia',
Journal of Modern African Studies, vol. 20, no. 3, 1982.

Shivji, Issa G., Class Struggles in Tanzania, Heinemann,
London, 1976.

Simmons, Michael and Obe, Ad'Obe, The Guardian Nigeria
Handbook 1982-3, Collins, London, 1982.

Smith, A.D., The Concept of Social Change: A Critique of the
Functionalist Theory of Social Change, Routledge and Kegan
Paul, London, 1973.

Smith, M.G., 'Historical and Cultural Conditions of Political
Corruption among the Hausa', <u>Comparative Studies in Society
and History</u>, vol. 6, no. 2, 1964.

Southall, T., 'Zambia: Class Formation and Government Policy
in the 1970s', <u>Journal of Southern African Studies</u>, vol. 7, no. 1,
1980.

Synge, R. (ed), <u>Africa Guide (1977)</u>, Africa Guide Company,
Saffron Walden, 1976.

Tignor, Robert L., 'Colonial Chiefs in Chiefless Societies',
<u>Journal of Modern African Studies</u>, vol. 9, no. 3, 1971.

Tignor, Robert L., <u>The Colonial Transformation of Kenya</u>,
Princeton University Press, Princeton, New Jersey, 1976.

Tordoff, William (ed), <u>Politics in Zambia</u>, Manchester
University Press, 1974.

Tordoff, William (ed), <u>Administration in Zambia</u>, Manchester
University Press, 1980.

Turok, B., 'Control in the Parastatal Sector in Zambia',
<u>Journal of Modern African Studies</u>, vol. 19, no. 3, 1981.

Wasserman, Gary, <u>Politics of Decolonization: Kenya Europeans
and the Land Issue 1960-1965</u>, Cambridge University Press,
1976.

Weber, Max, <u>The Theory of Social and Economic Organization</u>,
Oxford University Press, New York, 1947.

Werlin, Herbert H., 'The Roots of Corruption - the Ghanaian
Enquiry', <u>Journal of Modern African Studies</u>, vol. 10, no. 2,
1972.

White, Landeg, 'The Revolutions Ten Years On', <u>Journal of
Southern African Studies</u>, vol. 11, no. 2, 1985.

Williams, Gavin (ed), <u>Nigeria: Economy and Society</u>, Rex
Collings, London, 1976.

Williams, Robert J., 'Political Corruption in the United
States', <u>Political Studies</u>, vol. XXIX, no. 1, 1981.

World Bank, <u>Accelerated Development in Sub-Saharan Africa</u>,
Washington, D.C., 1981.

Wraith, Ronald and Simpkins, Edgar, <u>Corruption in Developing
Countries</u>, Allen and Unwin, London, 1963.

Young, Crawford, <u>Ideology and Development in Africa</u>, Yale
University Press, New Haven, 1982.

Index